THE
BEST
PERSON

FOR
THE JOB

MALCOLM BIRD

PIATKUS

To (in order of appearance in my life) –

Betty, Andrew, Melanie, Jonathan, Simon, Beverley,
Matthew, Abigail, Samuel, Joseph

© Malcolm Bird 1989

First published in 1989
by Judy Piatkus (Publishers) Limited
5 Windmill Street, London W1P 1HF

Paperback edition published 1990

British Library Cataloguing in Publication Data

Bird, Malcolm, *1932–*
    The best person for the job : where to find them and
    how to keep them
    1. Professional personnel. recruitment
    I. Title
    658.3'111

    ISBN 0–86188–924–X
    ISBN 0–86188–985–1 (pbk)

Designed by Paul Saunders
Edited by Kelly Davis

Typeset in 11/13pt Linotron Times by
Phoenix Photosetting, Chatham, Kent
Printed and bound by
Butler & Tanner Ltd, Frome, Somerset

CONTENTS

INTRODUCTION

THE purpose of this book is to provide a down-to-earth guide to recruiting and retaining the type of people a business needs. Large companies usually employ full-time professional staff to deal with this, but small to medium businesses are often unable to justify the cost of such specialists. General managers, company secretaries and other management people therefore have to spend part of their time on 'personnel' matters. And the time required is often found at the expense of other important aspects of their jobs.

This book should keep the time spent to a minimum by summarising what you really need to know in order to find and keep enthusiastic and productive employees. It will also be of interest to managers who have little or no direct involvement in recruitment but are concerned with leading and managing their workforce.

It is difficult, perhaps impossible, to imagine a business in which people are not the most important asset. In some businesses, such as insurance, accounting and publishing, the people in the business – and the skills they provide – are virtually the only asset. Even the manufacturing company which possesses valuable property in the form of buildings, land, raw materials, machinery and stocks of finished products is still entirely dependent on its people to use those assets to achieve profits.

Clearly, the value of employees is directly related to their abilities and experience. But it is the degree to which they are willing to apply their abilities and experience to the needs of the business that really defines their worth. In addition, people's abilities must be *relevant* to the particular needs of the business and applied in those areas of the business where they have the most beneficial effect.

The vital process of finding and keeping the right people involves an inevitable cost but it is not something to be treated as

1

an irritating chore by managers 'with better things to do'. Nor should it be allowed to deteriorate into a hit and miss affair. Any such approach leads to disappointment when the new employee turns out to be a dud, and puzzled head-shaking in the corridors of power when a key employee leaves for greener pastures. The wrong approach also leads to the sad or angry manager wondering why young Snooks, who was so hard-working and keen when he first started, now seems to do no more than the bare minimum and is on his way home the instant the factory hooter goes.

There are other symptoms of the company which has got it wrong. These include:

- many people leaving in the first few months of employment
- ever-increasing expenditure on recruitment
- a marked mediocrity in the longer-serving employees
- absence of initiative at lower levels and a tendency to resist change.

Above all, the company which has got it wrong will suffer a loss of profit. This is difficult to prove (causing complacency in the board room) because it is only possible to speculate on what the profit might have been if the company had got it right. However there is tangible evidence that a faulty system for finding and keeping the right people will put profits at risk. Let us suppose, for example, that an employee has left and the company wishes to find a replacement by advertising.

To advertise in the newspapers is likely to cost about £2,000. A manager earning around £25,000 per annum may spend time as follows to recruit the replacement:

- designing and placing the advertisement — 4 hours
- sifting through, say, 100 replies — 8 hours
- preparing a shortlist of about six applicants and arranging dates and times for interview — 4 hours
- replying to all the non-shortlisted applicants (standard letter) — 1 hour
- carrying out initial interviews — 6 hours
- discussing results with superiors and/or colleagues — 2 hours
- final interviews with perhaps two applicants — 2 hours
- taking up references — 1 hour

- general administration, e.g. organising
  medical examination, preparing employment contract, payroll and pension
  arrangements etc.   3 hours

  TOTAL: <u>31 hours</u>

The manager who does all this work – and the above list assumes that all went well and someone suitable was found first time round – will cost his or her employers about £500 per week in wages, plus about £200 per week in overheads such as pension contributions, national insurance payments and space and equipment costs. Added to which, the recruiter could have spent the same time on matters directly related to profit such as dealing with customers or supervising production. It is therefore not unreasonable to suppose that, in addition to the cost of the advertisement, a further £700 or thereabouts will be spent in management time. Some miscellaneous costs such as telephone and postage can be added, plus about £100 in secretarial time.

In summary the costs work out at:

	£
advertising	2,000
selection	700
secretarial	100
miscellaneous	<u>25</u>
TOTAL:	<u>2,825</u>

If the company sells its products at a gross profit of 10 per cent then more than £28,000 worth of sales must be made to cover the cost of this one recruitment.

Unfortunately it does not end there. Further, and possibly substantial, costs will be:

- the disruption caused by the loss of the departing employee and their knowledge of the business.
- the period of time during which the new employee is settling in and learning the job. Productivity and contribution can be low for many weeks.
- the effort involved in training the new employee. Whoever does the training will not be available for his or her normal work during training sessions.

3

- close supervision of the new employee (e.g. checking work done) during the early stages of employment.

What all these items cost is anyone's guess but the personnel director of a major British company expressed the following view:

> The provable cost of recruiting a supervisor or junior manager is unlikely to be less than £5,000. As a rule of thumb this amount should be doubled to allow for the disruption and other losses.

A further intangible but real cost lies in the adverse effect which an employee serving out a notice period can have on morale. Not only is the person leaving likely to be less than conscientious during the last few weeks or days ('If it goes wrong I won't be here when it bounces') but the leaver will probably also have an unsettling effect on other employees. At the very least, knowing that someone is leaving may cause other employees to think about greener pastures. At worst, the leaver will actively promote such ideas.

Frequent departures can also be bad for the company image. 'Every time I ring up XYZ company to place an order I find a new person in the sales department,' remarked a buyer for a London company. The buyer went on to complain that each newcomer had to be educated in his needs in terms of delivery arrangements, invoicing procedures and so on. Such situations tend to reduce confidence in the supplying company, particularly when an inexperienced newcomer makes a mistake.

Poor recruitment methods can clearly be a costly burden in both tangible and intangible terms. But the problem does not end there. Having acquired a good employee with potential, he or she needs to be quickly and effectively integrated into the business and their initial enthusiasm prolonged and sustained. This places a responsibility on management to learn and apply the techniques required to keep people happy and motivated, which is rather more complicated than just paying a good salary. It is possible to buy someone's presence in the company but it is not possible to buy their enthusiasm. The latter comes from treating them as what they are – people with hopes, fears and a whole range of other emotions.

This book also deals with these matters of motivation. It is certainly not a treatise on morality but it is nevertheless based on the principle that there is no conflict between the profit motive and treating employees as human beings.

A note on the use of 'he'

In a book of this kind it would be very cumbersome to keep using terms such as 'he or she', and 'his and hers'. For this reason, except where case histories or other requirements dictate, the masculine gender is used – and should be read as representing both genders. I do hope that women reading the book will not be offended by this stylistic decision.

1

WHAT DO WE WANT?

THE usual reaction to a valued employee handing in his notice is a display of hands thrown up in horror followed by a demand for a replacement as soon as possible. This reaction, while understandable, is not always the most constructive one.

Avoiding recruitment

Do we need to recruit at all?

The departure of an employee should never be regarded as a disaster, however much it may at first appear so. Every resignation should be viewed as an opportunity, bearing in mind the possibility that it may not be necessary to recruit a replacement at all.

The sales department of a medium-sized British company was divided into four sections. Each section, headed by a manager, dealt with a specific geographical area. One of the managers, deciding he could do better elsewhere, handed in his notice. At first this was treated as a major problem as no one in his team was considered ready to take over his role. In addition, finding a suitable outsider would be difficult and the section might be left leaderless for some time.

After a day or two the initial panic subsided and they began to consider whether they really needed four sections. The outcome, after much discussion and analysis, was a reorganisation of the whole department. This resulted in three sections instead of four, a better distribution of the workload, a more sensible and effective allocation of geographical areas and more cover for absences as a result of having larger sections. Once they thought about it they realised that things had changed since the four sections had first been set up and that the position had been maintained largely *because there were four managers in existence*. Losing one of them provided the opportunity to rethink and make a change – and save on payroll costs.

A resignation (or a retirement) might also provide opportunities to:

- delegate the work or share it out
- contract the work to an outside agency
- promote internally (with or without a recruitment at a lower level)
- mechanise the work (e.g. routine clerical work might be done by a computer)
- offer the work to an otherwise redundant employee
- above all, ask the question, 'Is this work really essential or is it something we can do without?'

Much of the agony involved in resignation or other unexpected departures of staff can be reduced or eliminated by thinking ahead. Many large companies employing thousands of employees use manpower planning techniques (see page 185) to reduce the cost and burden of dealing with staff losses, and also to anticipate the need to recruit for expansion or known retirements. The more elaborate computer-based systems used for manpower planning are not necessary in smaller organisations but the principles are the same.

Much time, effort and disruption can be saved in any company by adopting the following simple precautions:

- identify and train a successor for every key position
- prepare, say 12 months in advance, for someone's retirement
- constantly review organisational structures and the allocation of work to achieve the maximum flexibility and to limit the existence of watertight compartments.

A high degree of flexibility (e.g. people trained and willing to cross departmental boundaries) makes it much easier to reshuffle work, thus avoiding the need to recruit.

Can we promote internally?

There is one further aspect of vacancy-filling which should be considered before resorting to the external market. This is to look

7

closely *and objectively* at the people already available in the company. There is a tendency to dismiss the possibility of filling a vacancy by internal promotion. While there may be a lot to gain by recruiting fresh talent, there is also a lot to be said for promoting from within even if it involves a risk.

It is perhaps natural to say that young Fred has not been with us long enough or that Susie is not really sufficiently mature for the job. Such reactions should be examined objectively in the light of the following:

- we can be fairly sure of the degree of risk we are taking if we promote Fred or Susie. We will be less sure of an outsider, however good our selection methods.
- most people rise to the occasion if given the chance and a reasonable level of support.
- Fred or Susie can be motivated by being given a chance to get on.
- we know in advance the training that Fred or Susie will need. We may not be so sure with a newcomer.
- the job will be filled more quickly and continuity will be maintained. Fred and Susie are familiar with company structure, routines and customers.
- Internal promotions tend to be good for staff morale.

These then are some of the issues to be considered when we are faced with an apparent need to recruit someone. However, having said all this, at some time or other recruitment is bound to become unavoidable. At that point getting it right becomes the priority.

Preparing for recruitment

The first stage in preparing to recruit someone is to decide exactly what it is we want the newcomer to do. This need not necessarily be exactly the same as the work done by the outgoing incumbent and could, in some cases, be significantly different. What the incumbent of a job actually does is not necessarily what he should ideally be doing. Work and methods of working are substantially determined by the character, experience, abilities and preferences of the person doing the job.

A real-life case in point was the job done by Thomas, the general manager of the accounting department in a medium-sized company. Thomas died suddenly in his mid-50s after a lifetime in the company. During his years in the business the accountancy department had grown and Thomas had grown with it. The hand-ful of people Thomas had joined in his teens had increased to about 80 people and included two qualified accountants and a computer department. Thomas was not an accountant, nor had he trained in computer technology or management and, after his death, it was openly recognised that he had been out of his depth for some time. Ideally Thomas would not have acquired such a large or varied empire but there had been a reluctance, as the accountancy function grew in size and sophistication, to take any-thing away from him. Company loyalty to a long-serving employee prevented management from redistributing work and responsi-bilities.

Initially moves were made to look for a 'Thomas clone' but a review of the functions to be managed led to some second thoughts. It was realised that the accounting functions should be separated from the computing activities, the latter having been solely dedicated to book-keeping. Some alternative and potentially valuable computer applications had been neglected as a result of this. Under the new arrangement, the head of the computer department reported to a director whose responsibilities included non-accounting activities. And a statistical department was also moved to another, more appropriate part of the business.

The remainder of Thomas's department was reorganised to make better use of the two accountants, and an accountant with experience in tax and investment was recruited as the new boss. The result was a department better able to handle its primary function, led by a manager who brought with him some vital specialist knowledge.

By no means all recruitment situations require such elaborate consideration but if the right person is to be taken on *some* thinking will be necessary. This will lead to a job description – a document which is the foundation stone of intelligent selection yet is so often neglected.

The job description

Preparing a job description is *not* an exercise in time-wasting bureaucracy. It is the recruitment equivalent of an aircraft pilot's flight plan and just as essential. The job description does not describe the person you may want but, as the name suggests the job to be done. From this information you can deduce the type of person required. Essentially, it will be in two parts. The first part is a brief and fairly general statement of responsibilities and the second a more specific list of tasks to be done. Here is an example.

JOB DESCRIPTION

Job title:
Mail order clerk.

Responsibilities:
Reporting to the sales manager, to operate the mail order part of the business.

Duties:
1. To receive orders by mail and check that payment is enclosed and correct.

2. To pass payments (cheques and postal orders) to the accounts department.

3. To send despatch instructions to the warehouse and to monitor confirmation of despatch.

4. To maintain a record of orders received, showing category of customer, geographical area and quantity.

5. To prepare a monthly sales forecast and to liaise with the warehouse on stock levels.

6. To deal with customer complaints and to keep the sales manager informed of complaints.

If necessary such a job description might also include a statement of objectives to be achieved. This is valuable as a guide for a new recruit as well as helping to define the job to be done. For example, an objective for the mail order clerk might be 'To process all orders in not less than three working days from receipt of the order'. Such an objective (which should be sensible, relevant and achievable) not only defines the standards required but also indicates the time pressures which the clerk will experience. This in turn indicates something about the person required to do the job.

Similarly, the duties listed for the mail order clerk example will also indicate the type of person needed:

Duties	Qualities required
1. Receiving orders and checking that payment is correct.	Methodical, attention to detail, ability to work out prices, discounts etc.
2. Passing payments to accounts.	Methodical.
3. Sending instructions to warehouse and monitoring despatch.	Methodical, attention to detail.
4. Maintaining order records by customer, area and quantity.	Methodical, attention to detail.
5. Preparing monthly sales forecast and liaising with warehouse on stock levels.	Ability in arithmetic. Ability to communicate and gain co-operation.
6. Dealing with customer complaints.	Tact, courtesy, calmness under fire.

Clearly, the trouble taken in working out in some detail the type of work to be done pays off with an objective list of desirable attributes. Our mail order clerk will ideally be able to work methodically, deal with detail, cope with some mathematical calculations, work in a team (i.e. with the warehouse staff) and be courteous and able to deal constructively with disappointed customers.

There is no substitute for carrying out an analysis of this sort. It is not good enough to use the 'seat of the pants method' which, unless you are lucky or particularly shrewd, usually results in a vague, subjective and incomplete picture of the person required. This inadequate picture is normally the result of not consciously and methodically identifying and describing the actual tasks to be performed. It is also a fact that very few managers have a full, up-to-date and accurate knowledge of the work *actually* done by their subordinates.

'I didn't know that all this processing went on,' said the head of a purchasing department. 'I thought the computer did it all.' This statement followed the discovery that a potential recruit for the department would have to spend two or three hours at a computer terminal keying in the information the computer needed to do the job. The boss had been unaware that the previous incumbent spent a lot of time at a keyboard and that considerable keyboard skills were needed.

As this story shows, a vacancy occurring can be helpful and enlightening for a manager. It not only presents opportunities for useful change but also a chance to find out what really goes on. This knowledge may allow the manager to get rid of records, routines, forms and so on which the passage of time has made redundant. Out-of-date paperwork (in particular) has a tendency to persist unless firmly and positively challenged. The manager has to know what is being done in order to challenge it.

The person description

Preparing a description of the ideal person for the job (known variously by the jargon terms 'person profile', 'person description', 'candidate specification' and 'job-holder profile' – there are others!) is the second stage in the process. This description may include a number of attributes other than those directly indicated by the job description.

Age

A lot of time and money is wasted and a lot of human misery caused by age prejudice. Some would-be recruiters automatically take the view that anyone over the age of 30 is dying and anyone past 40 years is, for all practical purposes, already dead. Yet the same recruiter will often demand masses of 'essential' experience. This results in the type of advertisement sometimes seen in newspapers, asking for:

Qualified engineer with post-graduate management training (MBA) with a minimum of four years production management experience and knowledge of hydroelastic testing techniques acquired by practical application. Job costing and field survey experience is also highly desirable and fluency in German and French essential. Age in the range 25–30 years.

This fictional wording is based on a real-life advertisement which appeared in a British national newspaper. It is difficult to imagine how anyone can gain an engineering degree (a three- to four-year course) an MBA (one to two years), five years' production management experience and achieve fluency in two foreign languages by the age of 25. A really unusual person *might* just do it if he went straight into management from business school, did hydroelastic testing at weekends and learned languages at evening classes or in the bath. Even a 30-year-old would be hard-pressed to meet the requirements laid down.

The irony is that advertisements such as this are often placed by 50-year-old personnel directors at the behest of 50-year-old managing directors, none of whom would agree that age had reduced their energy or ambitions in the least. What is more, the age restriction means that all the first-class engineers in their 40s have been excluded – thus quite possibly excluding the best candidate for the job.

The converse age prejudice is exemplified by the people who believe that anyone under 30 years is likely to be lazy, feckless and irresponsible. Such a view is often combined with the notion that umpteen years of experience are needed for a relatively simple job. This particular attitude is often revealed by statements such as:

I did my 15-year apprenticeship before I was made a supervisor and no one can tell me that the job can be done properly without putting in the years needed to gain experience.

Age *is* important – and a lot too important to be subject to prejudice or egotistical notions about how much experience is needed. The facts are:

- there are very few genuinely lazy people. There are however lots of unmotivated people and these can be found in all age groups. (More will be said on this subject in Chapter 8.)
- generally, younger people are more appropriate where the job and the person are expected to develop and time is required for this.
- there are many jobs where older people are more suitable, including those where plenty of experience is *genuinely* necessary and those which offer little or no future development or promotion and in which an older person would be entirely content. The common example is the former housewife who,

having raised a family, is seeking a worthwhile occupation but does not want a stressful or over-demanding life.

● there are many energetic and ambitious older people, as can be seen not only in the board rooms of thousands of companies, but also among those who run their own private businesses. Some of the most effective management consultants, lawyers and research workers are also in their 50s, 60s or even older.

● the majority of young people, if treated properly, are hard-working and conscientious and want to achieve.

The golden rule when recruiting is to fit horses to courses. If the job is a dull dead end then this fact should be recognised and a person sought who would be happy in such a job – whatever their age. Alternatively, if the job requires imagination and creativity and has future potential someone appropriate should be sought. Their age should not matter although the older person will need to have enough working time left to meet the development needs of the job.

Whatever your requirements, do avoid making the mistake of excluding potentially suitable candidates by applying an illogical and unnecessary age restriction. In some countries (e.g. Canada and the USA) it is *illegal* to discriminate on the basis of age.

Academic qualifications

High turnover of staff in a large clerical department caused management to investigate the reasons. The main reason was exemplified by a 19-year-old member of the department who stated:

> I have three A levels and expected to find the work challenging. I found the work too easy and boring. It was much more difficult at school and I think I am wasting my A levels and my time.

The department concerned had made a positive decision only to employ people with a minimum of two A levels. They assumed that such people, having proven intelligence, would work more effectively. The fact that the work was dull, routine and required little intelligence was overlooked. The result was that the newcomers – who started full of enthusiasm – rapidly became disillusioned. The more energetic and ambitious ones decided to opt out and look for work which would stimulate them.

Once again the nature of the work should be carefully considered. Does the job description include tasks which require a high IQ and creative skills or does it list tasks which, once learned, make little demand on the intelligence? Some jobs such as accountancy, chemical analysis, surveying and aircraft design require someone with formal training and a qualification in the subject. In such cases the IQ level and qualification is determined for you.

However a vast number of jobs do not demand a formal qualification and some common sense and discretion is needed. While a PhD will probably not be required when looking for a filing clerk or a telephonist, we might be tempted to demand an A level in order to get a 'good' person for the job. This could well be a mistake unless the appointment leads *quickly* to some other type of work where A level ability really is needed.

An international chemical company adopted a policy of only employing university graduates in its sales force. This policy was dropped a year later when it was realised that a BA in history, archaeology or French did not guarantee an ability to sell or even an ability to learn *how* to sell. Not even the chemistry graduates were a universal success. Most of them felt that they were not using their technical knowledge as much as they would wish and moved on. In the meantime a lot of potentially good salesmen who did not have graduate qualifications were no doubt recruited by the competition.

Working hours and conditions
Will the job involve working anti-social hours or perhaps having to work late at short notice? It is no good complaining that an employee is a 9 to 5 clock-watcher if he is prevented from late working by travel problems, domestic responsibilities, a spouse's attitudes, or outside interests such as membership of a choir, the Territorial Army or an evening class.

Any potential problem should be recognised from the start and discussed fully with candidates. It is not reasonable (indeed it is asking for trouble) to reveal time demands *after* the employee has started. Nor is it reasonable or logical to expect employees to abandon all outside interests or responsibilities for the convenience of the business.

The same applies to holidays. In many businesses there are restrictions on holidays because of cyclical aspects of the trade. Many large retail stores will not permit any holidays to be taken during the run-up to the busy Christmas period or during the January or summer sales. Hotels may limit holidays to off-peak seasons such as early spring or autumn. Some companies limit the length of the holidays which may be taken and others will only allow a certain number of people to be away at any one time. The reasons for this type of restriction are normally well founded and the restriction reasonable but, once again, they should be recognised and explained to applicants (i.e. added to the job description) before the vacancy is filled.

Another important but often neglected aspect of working conditions is the environmental one. Some jobs are 'lonely' and the employee is cut off from human contact for long periods. The crane driver sitting in his cabin 100 feet above the building site will spend many hours with no one to talk to. So also will the stationery store clerk in the silent basement of an office block. The converse is the big open-plan office or the production line where there is constant human contact and sometimes plenty of noise.

Clearly there are people who will not suit one or other of these extremes and there are people who will prefer one of them. It is important to be aware of these 'social' aspects and allow for them in the recruitment process.

Career development

Quite apart from the questions of age and the development of a *job*, there is also the development of the *person*. Some companies recruit to fill newly created posts (e.g. as a result of company expansion or diversification) while others try to develop their own talent in order to fill the gaps from within. Similarly some companies groom younger people to replace retiring employees – often looking many years ahead.

Looking ahead is a particularly important part of preparing for recruitment. It can bring about a change in the idea about what sort of person is needed. And it helps to avoid last-minute searching around.

Too often, there is a mad last-minute rush to find out what a leaver does and how he does it. It is far better and less costly to identify the successor well in advance. This allows him to take on an understudy role to learn the job, thus bringing about a smooth handover. Such an arrangement can often be planned so far in advance that a new recruit – initially intended for a different role – can be selected with the eventual job in mind.

This implies that the person sought will, among
willing and able to learn the job of the outgoing per
to the primary role, have the attributes necessary to c
eventual position and be prepared to acquire any necessa
cal skills (e.g. by taking a study course wholly or partly in i
time).

In some cases an opportunity is presented by a known futu
departure to recruit a newcomer who will, in due course, bring
fresh skills and abilities to the job. This was the case with Thomas's
replacement (described earlier in this chapter) with the difference
that Thomas's death allowed no time for forward planning.

Fitting in

Everyone recognises the importance of compatibility. The damage
that can be done by a 'misfit' is well known and not infrequently
experienced. However a few minutes conscious thought will have a
marked effect. The decision as to which candidate will best fit in is
frequently left too much to 'gut instinct'. Of course, some degree
of subjectivity or instinct is probably inevitable but a little preparation can certainly make the process more reliable.

A useful tip is to write down the personality attributes of
someone already in the team who is a 'good fit'. The result is likely
to look something like this:

- naturally friendly and enjoys a joke
- willing to give others a hand when the going gets tough
- has leisure interests including sport
- non-smoker but not teetotal
- willing to take part in social club activities such as quizzes, the
  departmental darts match and collecting for charity.

Being aware of such desirable attributes means that a conscious
effort can be made to identify them in an applicant rather than
relying on a somewhat vague general impression.

Defining the right person for the job

Should we define the ideal person? The short answer is yes, even if
the chance of finding that person is remote. The value of defining
the ideal person lies in providing a target to aim at. However,
because the ideal person is rarely found, it is equally important to
specify the minimum which can be accepted.

Unless the minimum requirement is also clearly defined a great deal of money and effort may be wasted searching for the unattain-able. This is not infrequently followed by a panic-stricken decision, taken under pressure, in which someone is selected who is below the minimum – simply because the minimum was never defined.

Working out the minimum is often more difficult than working out the ideal. It is relatively easy to say that the ideal candidate will be fluent in Russian, German and Chinese, be able to type at 100 words per minute, have five years experience of exporting and be fully familiar with Department of Trade regulations relating to the sale and shipping of chemicals to Iron Curtain countries. The hard part is deciding whether someone with only a smattering of Russian, only two years exporting experience and no typing skills will do.

However there is no substitute for a cold sober look at what is an unavoidable minimum, and it can yield interesting results. It is not unknown, in practice, to discover that some of our supposed ideal attributes are not really necessary at all. They are often, for example, the attributes of the previous incumbent and not at all relevant to the job requirements as set out in the job description.

A London company had, for many years, employed only people with legal qualifications in a particular department. Most of the employees lasted two to five years before they resigned. And their replacements were always people with a similar legal training. For a long time the company ignored the relatively high turnover, until a shortage of legally qualified people began to make itself felt. After much fruitless and expensive searching for replacements the company managers stopped beating their breasts and focused their attention on the question: Why do people tend to leave after a relatively short time?

The reason which emerged was that very little of the work actually required advanced legal knowledge. People were leaving because they realised after a time that their legal skills were being under-used and their potential was not being developed. Although they were paid a salary appropriate to their qualifications they were nevertheless dissatisfied and frequently bored.

Looking back over the years, with the help of a long-since retired director, the company managers discovered that the whole idea of needing legally qualified people had started many years before. The first person to do the job in the 1930s had been a lawyer. From that time on everyone else had to be a lawyer! The company then took a more rational view of its needs and set minimum standards which allowed for the recruitment of people without legal qualifications but with the ability to learn the legal aspects of the job. The result was a resounding success, with reduced turnover, better morale, higher productivity *and* a lower wage bill.

The trap to be avoided therefore is to assume that the minimum requirements are the skills and qualifications of the existing or previous job-holder. And it is useful to separate the requirements into those which are essential and those which are desirable.

Keeping requirements specific

A final golden rule to be observed when putting together the person description is to be specific. Vague or general terms such as 'good education', 'accounting knowledge' or 'sales experience' should be qualified. These examples would be more clearly stated as, say, 'O levels in English, Maths and two other subjects', 'ability to work to trial balance' and 'not less than two years face-to-face selling to industrial companies.'

There are, of course, some requirements which are very diffi- cult or impossible to define. These include 'pleasant personality' or 'friendly manner', for example. However some attempt should be made to clarify such terms, however subjective it may be. Like all aspects of preparation for recruitment, every minute spent specify- ing such requirements will be rewarded and the chance of success proportionally increased.

Working from home – another option?

According to the *Industrial Relations Review and Report*, No. 430 (published in 1988) nearly a quarter of UK workers would be interested in working from home with a computer or word- processor. It is not likely that all those who would like to work in this way will have a job suitable for it but there will be some. The report showed that 'teleworking' is popular with both employees and employers and can help in recruiting and keeping staff. Employees working in their own home save time and money by avoiding daily travel and employers save the costs of providing office and other facilities.

In many cases a computer or word-processor need not be a prerequisite. Providing the work can be delivered and collected, a whole range of clerical jobs could be carried out off the company premises. If finding the right people is made easier by offering work at home it may be well worth considering.

Recruitment dos and don'ts

- **do** look upon every resignation, new vacancy or other reason to recruit as an opportunity. Take this opportunity to review the work to be done, the allocation of responsibilities and whether or not you really need to recruit someone at all.

- **do** prepare a job description. This in turn will help you accurately define the type of person you want. *Don't* treat this as a bureaucratic waste of time – it isn't and you can't afford not to do it.

- **do** prepare a written description of the person you should look for, based on the job description. This is something else you can't afford to neglect.

- **do** avoid irrational and potentially damaging age limitations and demands for unnecessarily high qualifications and levels of experience.

- **don't** forget to take the working conditions into account. Not everyone can work happily in a noisy shop and not everyone will survive eight hours a day all alone in the basement stockroom.

- **do** think ahead. The job may develop, placing increasing demands on the employee. Alternatively, you may want the employee to develop – or not.

- **do** take care over the 'fitting in' question. Consider carefully the type of people already in the company or department.

- **don't** rely solely on an 'ideal person' description. A minimum requirement should be defined as well.

- **do** keep your person description as specific as possible and avoid vague generalisations.

- **don't** forget the possibility of employing people working from home.

2

LOOKING FOR THE PERSON YOURSELF

PERHAPS the most common way for a company to start the process of finding new people is to place an advertisement in a newspaper or trade journal. The large job advertisement sections of many newspapers are a testament to the popularity of this method. However there are disadvantages as well as advantages, and alternatives which are often overlooked.

Advertising – the disadvantages

The first disadvantage of advertising in newspapers and the like is cost. A sizeable eye-catching advertisement can be very expensive, especially in the quality national newspapers.

Then there is competition. Your advertisement will appear alongside others which may appeal to the audience you are aiming at. This is particularly the case in specialist journals. An advertisement for a programmer in a computer magazine could be in competition with as many as 100 others.

Another consideration is image. The advertisement will not only be a statement of what you are looking for but will also give an impression of your company. The slightest mistake can be damaging and great care is needed in the wording. For example, some advertisers are prone to use lavish terms like 'world leaders in . . .' or 'dramatic growth . . .'. These terms are used to make the job sound more enticing and that is fine if the statement is true. In one group of 12 advertisements appearing in a British newspaper 10 of them were from companies describing themselves as 'leaders', 'dominant', 'market leaders' or similar. The reader can be excused for adopting some degree of scepticism when almost every advertiser claims to be *the* company in a particular industry.

A related issue is that of legal liability. A London company finding it difficult to secure specialist technical staff designed a series of advertisements which promised all kinds of exciting prospects. A number of staff were recruited as a result. But the whole thing turned very sour when some of the recruits found that their jobs were not as described. A series of legal actions for breach of contract and for misrepresentation were started. The company, after trying to ignore these actions, settled (expensively) out of court. They were also back to square one in the battle to find new staff.

The alternatives to advertising

Before discussing how to go about using advertisements it is worth considering some of the cheaper, and often easier, alternatives.

Personal contacts

Some companies offer bonuses to staff to introduce recruits to their companies. Existing staff can often find the person you are looking for – with or without the bonus inducement – and there are several advantages to this method. It is cheap and the potential recruit is unlikely to have an inaccurate picture of your company or the job since the employee introducing him will probably have given a warts and all account. The only danger is if your bonus offer is so high as to be a temptation to distort the facts. However this temptation would be counteracted by the prospect of living with a disappointed newcomer who would not be amused to have been misled.

There is also a better than average chance that the person introduced will fit in. Existing employees will be well equipped to find the type of person who is likely to fit in. They also know that if they introduce a troublesome recruit their colleagues will not thank them for it.

A bonus scheme to encourage employees to find recruits was introduced by the Post Office in Cambridge in 1988. Employees were offered £10 for each month that the recruit stayed at work – up to a maximum of £120.

Former employees

At a meeting to discuss staffing problems, the finance director of a British company declared that he would never take back a former employee. His stated reason was that anyone who had chosen to leave had no loyalty to the company. This attitude is long on injured pride and short on commercial acumen and logic. The reasons why someone left the company should be examined dispassionately and if there was a good reason (such as someone else offering a better career opportunity) then it makes every kind of sense to consider asking him to come back.

You will know the strengths, weaknesses and abilities of former employees and if they are what you need it is worth taking the trouble to find out what you must offer to get them back. This is often not just a question of more money. The person who left you may have done so to gain more responsibility, to escape a perceived block to promotion, to find more room for using initiative – or some other non-cash reason. You may now be in a position to give the former employee what he wants.

This method is also cheap, cuts out a lot of interviewing and decision-making and is safer. You know what you are getting if a former employee comes back. However, if he does come back you *must* keep any promises you make or you will lose him again.

Former rejects

The word 'reject' is somewhat harsh but it refers here to people who applied for a job with you but were turned down in favour of someone else. If six people are shortlisted and interviewed you will make an offer to the preferred candidate. That does not necessarily mean that all the other five are a dead loss. The difference between the winner and the runner-up may have been very slight. It is even possible that given six vacancies you would have taken on all six of the short-listed candidates.

Providing the earlier interviews were not too long ago, it could be worth contacting any of the rejects who may suit the present vacancy. Once again, this solution is a cheap one and has other advantages too. You already have details of the individual and have formed an impression of him. And the individual has some knowledge of you and your business.

Some people have argued that it is a waste of time going back to someone who has been turned down because of the disappointment and possibly bitterness the rejection may have caused. In practice, this is not a common reaction. Indeed, many rejected candidates are flattered and pleased to receive a carefully worded letter along the following lines:

> . . . and although we were not able to offer you the job advertised earlier we were nevertheless impressed by your record and potential.
>
> We now have another vacancy which we believe would be attractive to you and which would make good use of your experience . . .

Many people receiving such a letter will be pleased by the fact that you have remembered them and respond accordingly. The person who screws up the letter and throws it away shouting, 'Bastards, what do they take me for?' is not someone you should wish to employ in any case.

Job centres and other government agencies

Normally government agencies offer a free service and you may find just what you are looking for easily and cheaply. There is nothing to lose and everything to gain by contacting your local office. A company which moved one of its divisions from London to a town in East Anglia managed to fill álmost all its vacancies for office staff from the 400 or so people on the local professional and executive register. The cost was low and the enthusiasm of the recruits high.

Professional bodies

Some of the professions, associations and institutes run a job-finding service for their members. It can be well worth letting them know that you are in the market for a newly qualified accountant, an experienced engineer or whatever.

Schools, colleges and universities

Many of the major companies indulge in an annual 'milk round' of the universities, trying to capture the cream of the graduate output. This is often a very competitive process with the large companies laying on elaborate presentations, sometimes combined with 'inducements' in the form of expensive buffet lunches and ample alcohol.

Not only will smaller companies find it expensive to compete with household names backed by lots of cash, they may also consider it counter-productive. When students have been interviewed to obtain their reactions to such junkets, they are often found to be heavily laced with cynicism. As one physics graduate remarked, 'We went along for the food and the booze and an amusing hour.' The amusement was described as listening to a bunch of smoothies trying to describe a great future in a company which is known for its ruthlessness! Not at all what the MD had in mind.

The 'milk round' is therefore something to be treated with caution but a lower-profile approach can be effective. A British professional firm contacts appropriate officials at a number of universities prior to the final examinations, describing its likely vacancies and asking for this information to be passed to the more promising students in appropriate faculties. This is followed by quiet person-to-person contacts which do result in finding suitable people. It seems that this approach is more profitable than the big company circuses, which are very impersonal.

Similar low-key contacts with local schools and technical colleges can be useful, as can an 'open day' when students are invited to visit the company to see what it is like and talk to the employees. A friendly reception, an interesting explanation and an absence of pushy selling can produce results in future recruitments and in public relations generally.

Timing of contact with students is also important. According to a survey reported in *Personnel Management* (the journal of the Institute of Personnel Management) in January 1988, only 55 per cent of final year undergraduates had applied for a job by the end of the second term. In other words, a large number of students leave job applications until the end of their courses. At London University it was found that only 40 per cent had applied for jobs before Easter.

Advertising – how to go about it

Some of the alternatives to advertising may well give you what you want at lower cost. However it is likely that at some time or other you will have to advertise.

The essential elements

One experienced personnel director describes recruitment advertising as being all about:

Communicating Relevant Information

to an

Appropriate Audience

to produce a

Suitable Response

and

Favourable Results

at

Optimum Cost.

    The same director recommends writing the advertisement to the following pattern:

- the company
- the job
- the person
- and the conditions.

These are clearly the four key areas to cover in an advertisement because they give the job-seeker the essential information.

The company

The first golden rule is to say who you are – by name. Coy advertisements which avoid giving the company name are rightly treated with suspicion by many readers. A company which describes itself as 'well-known', 'leading' "substantial" 'famous' or the like, but does not say who they are, *appears* to have something to hide.

    In some cases the company name is kept out of the advertisement because they do not want existing employees to know they are advertising. This is a ploy designed to avoid trouble with any employees who might feel they should have the job – or for other internal political reasons. No intelligent person will take such a job in view of the resentment and opposition they would probably experience after joining.

    Having stated who you are, the advertisement should give a brief and accurate description of your company for the benefit of those readers (possibly the vast majority) who have never heard of you. This can be along the following lines:

> We are a small engineering company (100 employees) manufacturing widgets at our modern premises in Peterborough.

A statement such as this tells the reader:

- what you do   (engineering, making widgets)
- your size   (100 employees)
- and where you are   (Peterborough).

The reader is also informed that you are in modern premises. This removes any fears that your factory and offices are of the dreary Dickensian type.

The description of the company can also briefly include any other favourable points such as 'close to bus stops and railway station', 'well served by local transport' and/or 'ample free parking for employees'.

The job

The job description prepared earlier can now be used to pick out essential features which should be highlighted. Vague descriptions such as 'engineer' or 'clerk' should be avoided – there are 57 varieties of each of these jobs. It is the nature of the job which interests most people so extra care must be taken to describe it accurately, though this does not mean repeating the whole job description or explaining the obvious. For example, the term 'cost-accountant' does not need explanation. However, what the accountant will work on may need clarifying, e.g.:

> Cost-accountant to assist the chief designer in calculating expenditure on development projects of varying types in the engineering field.

This tells the reader that:

- the employee will assist (report to) the chief designer
- work will be on development projects
- the projects will vary
- the work is engineering-orientated.

This information is likely to appeal to a cost-accountant who would be attracted by assisting a senior person, likes variety and finds new products more exciting than routine matters. Knowing that the work is in engineering (not chemicals, building, transport or anything else), he can expect to be involved in parts-explosions, machine downtime calculations, metallurgical comparisons and the like.

If a particular skill is an *essential* part of the job description this should be explained to save the time and trouble of readers who do not fit – and to save yourself the burden of weeding them out. For example, the description of the cost-accountant's job could conclude:

> All project planning and development is carried out using computer terminals linked to a mainframe.

This makes it clear that the applicant will need to have computer terminal know-how and implies the use of spreadsheets and costing packages. Likewise, it should be made clear if the job involves travel (and to what extent), anti-social hours or any other significant aspects identified in the job description.

The person
The main features of the person description should now be briefly listed, taking care to avoid the mistakes mentioned in Chapter 1, e.g. being unnecessarily demanding or restrictive in respect of age or qualifications.

The conditions
Ideally the salary will be stated. Many advertisers are reluctant to say anything about salary and thereby lose the interest of a substantial proportion of readers. Other advertisers take refuge in expressions such as 'salary negotiable', 'highly negotiable' and, even more puzzling, 'upper quartile'.

You must have some idea of how much the job is worth to you *and* the going rate in your area. If not, some thinking and research needs to be done. It is only at very senior levels that 'salary negotiable' or 'according to experience' is acceptable. Young or junior people rarely have the confidence or know-how to negotiate a salary and the majority will skip the advertisement and go on to the next.

In one real-life case the advertisement stated 'five-figure salary'. Although this gave a range of £10,000 to £99,999 the selected candidate found at the interview stage that it meant the bottom figure. When told this he walked out, never to return. He took the view, perhaps understandably, that someone had been trying to pull a fast one.

There may be other benefits on offer. If so, they should be mentioned, as their value to the person you are looking for could be considerable. Among the possibilities are: luncheon vouchers, subsidised canteen, health insurance, life insurance, pension scheme, discounts, bonuses and *the* perk with pulling power – a company car.

Remember that you are advertising in a competitive market – often a strong job-seeker's market – where every advantage you can offer should be stated. Advertisers should not make the mistake of taking a 'superior' view and declaring that the person wanted will be the type who values long-term career prospects and will not be interested in benefits. This attitude is entirely unrealistic and is likely to result in fewer applications. There may be people who give greater weight to long-term prospects but they still have to live in the meantime. Cheap lunches and discounts on goods can make the short term much more attractive and form part of the reward that everyone seeks.

Other *significant* conditions should also be mentioned, such as overtime, holiday entitlement and sports or social activities.

It is a fact that a clear description of the reward package – salary and perks – will narrow down the field of applicants to those who are genuinely in the market at the level indicated. There is nothing more time-wasting or depressing than to find out at interview stage that what you have to offer is not enough for an attractive candidate. So, to get the maximum number of applications from the stratum you are looking for, give them the facts.

These then – the details of the company, job, person and conditions – are the essential requirements. They will also directly influence the way the advertisement is designed.

Designing the advertisement

To a large extent, the layout and style of the advertisement will determine whether the person you are looking for actually reads it or merely skips over it. And the design will in turn depend partly on where the advertisement is situated. If it is to be large and appear in a block along with other large advertisements there is more room for, say, an eye-catching heading. If, for cost reasons, it will be among the small ads space will be a limiting factor.

29

Catching the eye of the reader can be achieved by:

- taking up a lot of space. This is effective but expensive.
- using graphics, such as those used by companies in the aviation world. These normally include racy-looking aircraft dashing across the advertisement. While certainly eye-catching, graphics add considerably to the cost.
- using a bold headline. This is a cheap alternative but since almost every advertisement will have a bold headline the effect is somewhat reduced. It is more a case of 'If you don't do it you have no chance at all.'
- using an unusual headline. This is not expensive and, with a little effort expended in thinking it out, can be very successful.

A warning about headlines in job ads was given in a survey report produced by the consultants Price Waterhouse. A summary published in *Personnel Management* in November 1988 included the comment, 'Catchy or cryptic headlines in recruitment advertisements get the thumbs-down from executive job-seekers . . .'

Wording the advertisement

Having captured the interest of the reader the rest of the wording must hold it. Not every job-seeker or person idly scanning the job page need be attracted. The aim is to hold the interest of the specific type of person you are looking for.

This does not require brilliant prose or the use of esoteric techniques known only to the copy writers employed by advertising agents. There is no magic system – just the application of common sense to the work already done in preparing the job description and the person description. If the message is clearly *relevant to them* the right people will read the advertisement right through and seriously consider responding. To achieve this the content should include the following:

- the job title or an equivalent. (Ensure that the job title is specific enough to be meaningful. Problems can also arise if you use rather obscure internal job titles. For example, you may call your fork-lift truck drivers 'stock movement operatives' – a term which requires some explanation.)
- a concise and clear description of the ideal and minimum candidate.

Note 1: Having read this far, all the unsuitable people should have abandoned your advertisement while those to whom the job is relevant should still be interested.

- the type and size of the company and where the job is located.

Note 2: Those readers who are not attracted to your kind of company and/or are excluded by the location will probably drop out at this stage. You will now be left with those to whom your company, the job and its location are of interest. This interest needs to be converted into a desire to apply or make further enquiries, and this should be achieved by the remaining items:

- the salary and other benefits.
- future prospects – if applicable.
- any other feature likely to be attractive to the type of person you are looking for. Security may be such a feature or, alternatively, opportunity to travel.
- a *friendly* invitation to apply, with simple easy-to-follow instructions on how to do it.

The last item is particularly important. Many otherwise interested candidates will be put off by complicated or over-formal demands. There is all the difference in the world between:

> Applications must be received at this office no later than 1st July and must be accompanied by a full curriculum vitae and a statement showing why you are suitable for the position advertised.

and

> If this job looks like the one you are searching for please give us a call on 753 8854. We will be pleased to answer any questions you may have and will send you a brief application form. If more convenient just drop us a line with your personal details.

Advertising pitfalls

There are a number of traps which advertisers can fall into. The major ones are covered below.

House advertising

As I have mentioned, any announcement made by your company will have some influence on the company image. However this does not mean that a recruitment advertisement should do the job of advertising your company or your product. Yours may be the greatest company ever, and provide the most amazing product since the wheel was invented, but a few words will do to establish who and what you are. The objective is to find a new employee, not to impress the world of finance and investment. Concentrate on the person, not the company.

Over-formal presentation

Some advertisements are unbelievably boring. This is usually due to their use of almost Dickensian prose heavily laced with job ad jargon. For example:

> 'This old established concern seeks suitable applicants for a vacancy in its research division. Applicants possessing appropriate qualifications are invited to communicate with us with a view to . . .'

The style should be friendly, appropriate to the audience being addressed and use everyday English.

Breaking the law

In most western countries there are laws to prevent discrimination when offering jobs. The legal position should be thoroughly checked and the advertisement draft carefully examined to ensure that the law is complied with. It is all too easy to overlook an *implication* in your wording that preference will be given to one sex or that certain types of people will be excluded. It is too late when faced with a legal action to plead, 'But we didn't mean that.'

Jokes, gimmicks and dynamism

When looking for young sales staff it may be fine to use the 'whizz-bang' style of advertising in which there is much use of terms such as 'fast-moving', 'dynamic', 'go-getting' and 'exciting'. Such advertisements may well appeal to young firebrands eager to earn a fortune in commission but they are not likely to appeal to anyone else.

Similarly, jokes and puns – sometimes used in an effort to appeal to younger people – are not likely to be successful with those who take their jobs seriously. This style of advertising may have its (limited) place but should be treated with caution.

Finalising the wording

Having drafted, checked, re-drafted and checked again, you should have an advertisement which will work. 'Should have' because if you have followed all the steps described in this chapter you will have followed a logical process. However you can still be wrong if only because the words you have chosen seem right to you while the audience you are aiming at may react very differently.

A useful test is to find someone of the same age group and type as your target audience and ask them to comment on it. In some cases the opinion of existing staff is particularly helpful, especially if there is someone doing the same job as the one to be advertised. Such people may well have a more accurate idea of what features of the job need to be emphasised. If suitably encouraged, they can also tell you if you have painted too rosy a picture or made claims or statements which could cause trouble later.

The final stage of re-reading and reconsideration is just as important as any of the preceding stages and should not be rushed. However, at some point you will be satisfied with your wording and can move on to the next stage.

Placing the advertisement

There is a vast choice of media available to the intending advertiser, ranging from the wholly unsuitable to the appropriate. The choice will be largely determined by the type of job involved. The chart on the next page is a general guide to the choice of medium, based on job type but, for the moment, ignoring costs.

Advertisements have also been successful on local radio or television but usually only where blue collar workers are needed. The cost is relatively high so this choice of medium is normally only suitable for the major employer with lots of vacancies to fill.

The chart overleaf is of course only a general guide and other factors must be taken into account. Technical and trade journals offer a selective readership and can be particularly helpful in finding certain specialists such as accountants, computer staff, engineers, scientists and insurance staff. And local newspapers (both daily and evening) are especially useful for reaching people in selected areas.

There are, in addition, two traps to be avoided. The first is an assumption that 'a better class of newspaper will produce a better

Medium	Manual	White collar	Management
National Sunday papers (quality)	Poor	Fair	Good
National Sunday papers (popular)	Good	Fair	Poor
National dailies (quality)	Poor	Fair	Good
National dailies (popular)	Good	Fair	Poor
Local weeklies	Good	Good	Fair
Local dailies	Good	Good	Fair
Evening papers	Good	Good	Poor
Technical journals	Fair	Good	Good

class of candidate'. The better class candidate is the one most suited to the vacancy to be filled and he may not be a quality paper reader. The second is another assumption – that the right candidate will read the same journals as the author of the advertisement. This may be true but is often not. You need to do some realistic thinking about the type of person you want and where he is likely to look for a job.

Cost

There is no such thing as a 'cheap failure'. All failures are expensive since they are a *total* loss, costly in time and effort, and costly in delaying recruitment. So it is not a good idea to go for the cheapest just for the sake of 'saving money'.

In advertising, as in other activities, we almost always get what we pay for. A full-display advertisement will cost more than a semi-display but, all other things being equal, it will attract more attention and gain more responses. A budget should be set and the necessary resources allocated to achieve the objective. Anything less is trusting to luck and asking for trouble.

The actual price you will have to pay for various sizes (and possibly according to the position) of your display can only be determined by asking the journals you are interested in. Generally, national newspapers are the most expensive, followed by provincial newspapers, then local newspapers, then professional and trade journals, and finally free newspapers.

As a rule of thumb, it is probably not worth advertising in the national papers (Sunday or daily) for any job with a salary of less than £15,000.

Timing

A lot of nonsense is talked about the timing of advertisements for jobs. While it is certainly true that experience shows Saturday to be a bad day, there are pros and cons to other times. For instance it has been argued that the summer holiday season is a bad time. If some advertisers believe that to be true then you will have less competition if you place your ad right in the middle of the summer. It may also be that people on holiday have time to read the advertisements and that many take stock of their lives and consider a change when away from work for a couple of weeks. Some people's experience suggests that advertising close to public holidays can be unproductive but even this has been challenged.

Some newspapers have particular days for particular types of job and others have days on which more than the normal number of advertisements are featured. It seems to be the case that many job-seekers will concentrate on the designated days – particularly those devoted to particular types of job. Although you will face some competition from other advertisers on the designated days, on balance it seems desirable to go for them.

Keeping a record

It is a useful exercise to keep a record of the results of your advertising efforts. Over a period you may try, say, one or two local newspapers and a trade journal. Make a note of the costs and results achieved from each. Figures worth recording are:

- the cost
- the number of responses
- and the percentage of good responses, i.e. those which are serious, relevant and worthy of consideration.

Over a period of time this information will become valuable as a guide to the best advertising media for your particular business and the type of people you employ. If you can share this information with one or two friendly companies near you then quite a lot of valuable data will be accumulated – to the benefit of all.

An example of the value of sharing the experience of others – and a good illustration of the danger of making assumptions based on hunches was given in the magazine *Mind Your Own Business* (November 1987). Reporting on the experiences of Pitney Bowes in Ireland the magazine stated:

> Like most major companies . . . Pitney Bowes had been taking large advertisements . . . They soon realised that when the paper comes out on Friday, young people look down the columns ignoring the large expensive-looking advertisements . . .
> They move to the small classified ads to look for something they can identify with.

The magazine went on to report that Pitney Bowes shifted from the £2,000–£2,500 advertisements to the small ads. Considerable savings were made in the process.

The non-traditional media

It is perhaps natural to think first of the traditional media to place an advertisement. It can be argued that the majority of job-seekers will turn to the usual pages of the usual newspapers and magazines. However a recent trend is to place job ads in less traditional places such as the Sunday colour supplements.

This raises the question: 'Why not place an advertisement in a non-traditional medium which is likely to be read by the type of person sought?' There are many magazines, for example, aimed at different segments of the population, including do-it-yourself enthusiasts, gardeners, young women, film and theatre buffs and many others. A careful choice could result in your advertisement being read by a significant number of the type of person you are seeking – without so much (or any) competition from other advertisers.

Advertising dos and don'ts

- **do** consider the alternatives to advertising:
  personal contacts
  former employees
  former (rejected) applicants
  job centres

professional bodies
schools and colleges.
You may save yourself a lot of time and money.

- when advertising **do**:
say who and what you are
describe the job
describe the person wanted
quote the salary and other benefits.

- when advertising **don't** use cryptic or jokey headings – studies have shown that these put many job-seekers off.

- **do** remember that your primary purpose is to advertise for the person you want. **Don't** end up with an advertisement for the company or its products instead.

- **don't** use old-fashioned boring wording and go easy on the jargon.

- **do** check your advertisement draft carefully for accuracy and legal requirements. **Don't** be afraid to ask your existing employees to comment on it – you could learn a lot!

- **do** choose your medium with care, bearing in mind the kind of person you are looking for. The 'better class' media may not produce what you really need.

- **don't** skimp on costs. Be realistic – there is no such thing as a cheap failure.

- **do** keep records of the results of using different media and types of advertisement. This could save you money in the future.

- **do** think seriously about advertising in non-traditional media.

3

LOOKING FOR THE PERSON WITH OUTSIDE HELP

THE main reasons for using outside help in the form of agencies, selection consultants and headhunters are to save you time and to employ expertise you may lack. Whether or not you will save money is a moot point, as the fees can be high. However if you find the person you really want, using a minimum of your own time, this could represent a cash saving. It depends on how you value your own time.

What kind of help is available?

The first thing to be clear about is what forms of outside help exist. A number of terms are used to describe the businesses concerned. For example, some companies call themselves 'bureau' while others prefer 'agency', and as you go further up the market you may hear various fine-sounding titles such as 'search consultant', 'selection consultant', 'recruitment consultant' and even 'human resource consultant'. At least the use of the word 'consultant' is fairly standard. Essentially these firms fall into three broad categories.

Agencies

These businesses operate somewhat along the lines of the old labour exchanges. They invite job-seekers either to register with them or to respond to advertisements which are normally written on cards and placed in the agency window.

At the same time they note the needs of their clients and, from the job-seekers who come to them, will try to match people to jobs. Agencies vary in the care and expertise applied to this matching process. Some will interview job-seekers in depth, others will not. Some will check track-record and references, others will not.

Having found an apparent match, agencies will normally contact the potential employer and provide more or less comprehensive details of the job-seeker. Should the employer accept the person sent to them, a fee – normally a percentage of the first year's salary – is payable to the agency.

Generally, businesses such as these deal at the lower end of the salary scale. The great majority of the jobs they handle will be clerical, manual and other non-executive appointments.

Selection consultants

The selection consultant will normally have a number of job-seekers on record, advertise if necessary, interview likely candidates and select a shortlist for interview by the employer. The consultant will then arrange the interviews and provide a comprehensive report on each shortlisted candidate. This report will not only provide details of background, career, qualifications and the like but will also include the consultant's own assessment.

The fee for this work will be a percentage of the salary agreed – 15 to 25 per cent is the normal range but as much as 33 per cent has been asked for by some consultants. In return for this not inconsiderable fee the consultant provides:

- the benefit of his knowledge of the market and any existing contacts he has
- a professionally handled advertising campaign (if necessary)
- initial screening, interviewing and fact-finding
- and finally a selection of potentially suitable people.

Most consultants will also be prepared to discuss and advise you on potentially tricky questions such as what salary to offer, age range and essential experience for the job.

Selection consultants usually work at executive level and look for technical experts (e.g. engineers), junior or middle managers and various specialists such as computer systems analysts. Some consultants concentrate solely on a particular profession or business field such as insurance, scientific research or banking.

Headhunters

These are the people who offer their services to recruit the top level of management and key specialists. Headhunters (or 'executive search consultants' as they prefer to be called) may well be contracted to fill a job for which there are only, say, 20 suitable people in the whole country.

An air of mystery – if not magic – has grown up around the headhunting business and, in consequence, it has received much media attention. But it is actually not the typical way in which senior or specialist recruitment is achieved. In a sense headhunters are brokers who, having been given the job of finding someone, will identify a likely prospect and try to talk him into it. The work is done under cover and advertising is rarely involved. How well the headhunter can cover the market depends on his contacts and his ability to carry out research. Some are very effective, others less so.

The tendency from around 1985 has been to employ headhunters for the very high salary jobs. On the face of it, this is not very sensible. A high salary does not in itself mean that advertising is out of the question or that the person required is necessarily hard to find. For example, there are plenty of highly paid insurance brokers in the City of London. Frankfurt and Zurich have a sizeable population of highly paid banking experts and downtown Manhattan is awash with financial whizz-kids.

In many cases there is no reason why such people should not be recruited by the do-it-yourself method or by using a competent selection consultant. If, on the other hand, you are genuinely looking for a very rare animal, the headhunter may be the answer. Then again, if you are in an industry where there are a few very special people you will probably already know who they are and can ring them up yourself.

Headhunters' fees are normally in the 30 per cent of salary bracket. This is the so-called 'contingency fee system' in which no money changes hands unless a suitable candidate is found and recruited. Not surprisingly, many headhunters prefer a 'retainer system' in which they are certain of a hefty proportion of the total fee even if they fail to deliver the goods.

Which kind of help to choose?

Assuming that you have reasons (perhaps shortage of time) for not doing it yourself, the following table is a general guide to the type of outside help to go for.

Type of service	Indications
AGENCY	• lower-level jobs • no apparent shortage in the market • employer willing to do much of the selection
SELECTION CONSULTANT	• middle to senior level jobs • expert help needed and employer not willing to design advertisements or interview widely
HEADHUNTERS	• when only a few people can fill the job and these are hard to locate • when secrecy is essential

Making a careful choice is of prime importance, as evidenced by the horror stories passed around from time to time and the results of studies. It was reported in *A Study of Industry's Use of Headhunting* by Ian Ashworth and Associates (1988) that 38 per cent of 150 companies questioned had, at some time, been dissatisfied with the services of headhunters. This high level of dissatisfaction was caused by, among other things, failure to understand the client's needs, failure to keep the client informed, expense and slowness.

Agencies have also come under fire – particularly for charging unreasonably high fees. In a study of 672 personnel and recruiting line-managers reported in the January 1988 edition of *Personnel Management* it was stated that 81 per cent considered that agencies charged too much.

Though many of these tales of woe are apocryphal there is at least one which is true and offers a warning. A company in London recruited a word-processor operator through an agency. After a puzzling first day it was found that the new employee had almost no ability to use a word-processor. Her previous experience had been as a sewing machine operator! A simple test given by the employing company before taking the person on would have revealed the agency's error.

The vast array of agencies, consultants and headhunting firms (each numbered in their hundreds) does not make the choice any easier. Nor is it safe to assume that the big names will suit you best. Some sort of logical procedure is necessary if the hazards of trial and error are to be avoided. The following steps are recommended:

- choose, say, three companies in your area. This initial choice could be virtually at random if you are starting from scratch and will probably be based largely on the convenience of their location. You will want to talk to them – preferably face to face – so it pays to make it easy.

- ask each company to provide you with their brochure or something else which gives a clear statement of their terms of business and field of expertise.

- having studied the information provided, talk to a *senior* representative of the company and ask the following questions (if they are not fully and adequately answered in the literature):

  – What are the charges and how is billing done?

  – What precisely is done for the fee?

  – How much time and effort are they prepared to put into understanding your needs and, in due course, keeping you informed?

  – What information do they keep (e.g. trends in wage rates) which they are prepared to pass on to you? Will this information be provided free of charge?

  – How long has the company been in business and what experience do the principals have?

  – Will any particular person look after your needs and, if so, what are the qualifications and experience of this person?

  – Is the company a member of a recognised trade association which imposes a code of conduct on its members? What are the main provisions of any such code of conduct?

  – Do they offer any back-up services which might help you such as recruitment brochure design, application form design or training material?

- having asked these questions, ask them for the names of clients to whom you may apply for references. This may be refused either on the grounds of confidentiality ('We never disclose our clients' names') or just refused. In either case drop them from your list. If they are genuinely concerned about client confidentiality they can easily ask their clients' permission to disclose names – and should be willing to do so.

- telephone any clients whose names are given to you. Don't write – a telephone conversation is much more revealing.

- check with any other possible client companies where you have contacts who may be able to give you information.

- make your choice on the basis of all that you have learned, give them a job to do and monitor them closely. The monitoring should include impressions of the first recruit found for you. Was he properly interviewed, tested – or whatever was appropriate? Did he find the process friendly and enjoyable? Would *he* recommend using them again?

The hope is that you will have started a long-term, pleasing and mutually beneficial association. If you are not so fortunate cut your losses and try again with another company.

Working with the agency or consultant

A selection consultant was asked what kind of clients he most liked working for. His answer boiled down to the following:

- clients who carefully work out and discuss with him what sort of person they are looking for (and avoid changing their minds halfway through the selection process).
- clients who constructively discuss with him his proposed advertisement, its wording, design and choice of medium. (One of his nightmares was the client whose chairman insisted on personally reviewing every advertisement, delayed progress – sometimes drastically – and argued destructively about every word and comma.)
- clients who keep appointments arranged with shortlisted candidates, don't keep candidates waiting and prepare properly for the interview.
- clients who make up their minds for or against candidates in reasonable time – and before the candidates have been snapped up by someone else.
- clients who keep to their word about salary and other job conditions and don't try to change them at the last minute.

The implication in these attributes of the good client are obvious. The same rules apply to working with a supplier of recruitment services as for the purchase of other services or goods. It should never be an adversarial activity but one based on mutual respect and co-operation. This is the only way to achieve the best results.

Dos and don'ts of using outside help

- **do** take some trouble in researching which agency or consultant will best suit *your* business.

- **do** follow a methodical process in selecting your agency or consultant and don't fail to ask penetrating questions.

- **do** contact previous clients for references.

- **do** be prepared to give an adequate briefing.

- **don't** make unrealistic demands. For example, allow adequate time for the job to be done properly.

- **do** listen to the advice given to you. It should be remembered that the provider of the service is recruiting people all the time. It is therefore likely that he will have a better knowledge of pay rates, the best media to use and what appeals to the various age groups.

- **don't** try to argue fees down to a non-economic level.

- **do** pay your bills on time. This could get you favoured treatment the next time you want to recruit.

4

ENCOURAGING APPLICATIONS AND DEALING WITH THEM

FROM time to time every one of us is astonished at how difficult a seller of goods or services can make it for a would-be buyer to purchase his product. A director of a leading British company wanted to buy a product from another leading British company. According to the seller's advertisement a telephone call was all that was needed. The reality was very different!

The director made his phone call and, after long delays, was asked a whole series of questions – many of which appeared irrelevant. In addition these questions were asked *before* the buyer had stated his needs. After about 20 minutes the order was 'accepted', subject to satisfactory financial references *and* payment in advance. The director pointed out that his company had purchased from the selling company on several occasions over a number of years. The man at the other end of the line was unmoved. Since *he* had no record of the previous transactions on *his* computer screen, references and cash had to be provided. The director took his business elsewhere.

Similarly, obstacles placed in the way of would-be applicants for a job can cause them to take their business elsewhere. Chapter 2 mentioned the need for friendly and simple application instructions. This requirement must now be examined more closely.

The typical application process

The following stages are all too common:

- applicants are invited to write in with personal details.
- the applicant replies with a letter – or a curriculum vitae – providing details.

- two to three weeks pass while the recruiting company reviews the letters and the curricula vitae they have received.
- the applicant, beginning to wonder if his letter has gone astray or the company has gone bust, receives a four-page application form. This form asks for all the information he has already provided. He wearily completes the form and sends it in.
- a further two or three weeks go by before the applicant receives a letter calling him for interview at impossibly short notice.
- the applicant telephones, is passed from one person to another and is eventually told, 'I'm sorry but I cannot give you another date for the interview as Mr Snooks is in a meeting and cannot be disturbed.'
- the candidate gives up and looks for a job elsewhere.

The above scenario is not in any way exaggerated. It is taken from real life and does not include some even more unsatisfactory practices which are known to take place in the recruitment world.

Every applicant is entitled to courtesy and consideration and the best ones will not put up with long delays, lack of consideration or bureaucratic nonsense.

The situation described above can be avoided firstly by achnowledging *every* application promptly. Word-processing makes it entirely possible for the acknowledgcment to be in the form of a pleasantly worded individual letter. (A pre-printed card is not good enough.)

Then, if there is any delay, a brief letter along the following lines should keep the applicant interested and reduce any anxiety:

> . . . we are interested in your application. Please be assured that we have not forgotten you and will be in touch again as soon as possible. In the meantime we apologise for the delay and hope it has not caused you any worry or incon-venience . . .

In addition, you should not insist on having an application form filled in unless the candidate is at least shortlisted for interview and preferably not even then. (The question of application forms is discussed in more detail later in this chapter, page 52.)

Finally you should adopt an understanding and flexible attitude to dates, times and places for interviews. The applicant may have great difficulty in taking time off for interviews and may be putting his present job at risk. The more understanding recruiters will be prepared to offer an evening appointment for people with difficulties and, subject to the time pressures on filling the job, will offer alternative dates and times.

There will almost certainly be some applicants who are clearly not suitable for the job on offer. This, if apparent from their letter, should result in a prompt and polite refusal letter to put them out of their misery. Bear in mind that many people could be anxiously waiting for your reply – and may be postponing making applications elsewhere until they hear from you.

The appalling and all too common practice of totally ignoring apparently unsuitable applicants should be avoided like the plague. Quite apart from questions of ethics and courtesy, you will create 'an enemy' every time your company treats someone badly. Who knows where these enemies may end up? Possibly as people to whom you would one day like to sell your product or service. Anecdotal evidence suggests that it is the larger companies who tend to act in this way. Presumably their size makes them feel invulnerable when in fact every business needs all the friends it can get – and no enemies.

The 'ideal' application process

Accept well-written letters and curricula vitae as the equivalent of an application form. Do not ask for additional information unless it is absolutely unavoidable and, if you do need more information, limit your request; in other words, do not send a form which requires the applicant to repeat everything he has already told you.

Weed out those applicants you are definitely not interested in and notify them without delay.

Write to those you wish to interview suggesting a time, date and place – and offering to make changes if required. At the same time give the applicant the full name and telephone number of a person with the *authority* to rearrange appointments if necessary.

Include more details of your business in your letter. Applicants may need to know more about your company than you could tell them in the advertisement. Don't make the mistake of thinking that the whole world knows your business as well as you do.

A copy of the job description is a 'must' and an organisational chart highly desirable. The job description – which will be more comprehensive than the advertisement wording – will give the applicant a better understanding of what you are looking for. It should also make him realise, where such is the case, that he is not suited to the job and should withdraw his application. This will save both his and your time.

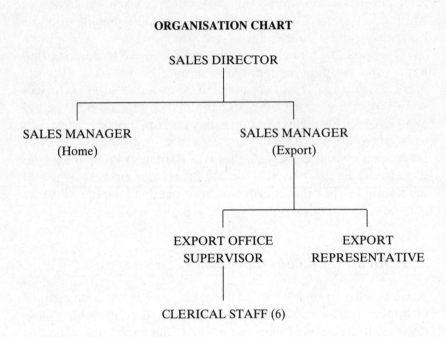

ORGANISATION CHART

SALES DIRECTOR

SALES MANAGER
(Home)

SALES MANAGER
(Export)

EXPORT OFFICE
SUPERVISOR

EXPORT
REPRESENTATIVE

CLERICAL STAFF (6)

The organisation chart will show the candidate how the job fits into the overall hierarchy and will give an indication of its status. This is also important because, however well-designed the advertisement may be, the candidate's perception of the job's status and seniority may be different from yours. This is particularly the case with jobs entitled 'General Manager' or 'Supervisor'. In some companies and industries a general manager is a much more responsible person than in others. The same applies to supervisors.

If the applicant withdraws as a result of seeing the organisation chart – or he queries the reporting structures in some way – you should regard this as a sign that your system is working. Selecting someone for a job is never a one-sided process. It is in the interests of both the empoyer and potential employee to get it right and the applicant should be allowed to play a full part. Indeed, the more intelligent and switched-on candidates will insist on being given the information to enable them to decide whether the job is right for them as well as whether they are right for the job. The two things are not necessarily the same.

The company annual report and product brochures will also be helpful to the candidate. They will help him assess what sort of business you are running. The information in these documents will also give him leads to 'check you out'. A sensible candidate will do this by making enquiries about your standing in the industry, your professional and ethical reputation and the quality of your product or service. He will also try to find out what present and former employees think of you. Do not resent this type of enquiry. It is all part of a screening process to ensure that the people you interview actually want a job with *you*, as opposed to just wanting a job. The difference has implications for the level of commitment the eventual recruit will demonstrate.

Sifting the applications

Depending on a variety of circumstances you may receive a flood of applications, a handful or, at worst, none at all. A small number of replies, while perhaps disappointing, at least makes the sifting process quicker.

Let us assume, however, that you have about 50 applications in the form of letters or curricula vitae. Once again a methodical approach is necessary to do an efficient job of sorting them out. Some may be 'self-rejecting' and these could include:

- applicants who are far outside the age range.
- applicants who do not remotely match the type or extent of experience you are looking for.
- applicants whose level of literacy falls well below that required.
- the occasional 'nutcase' application. One of these received by a British company was from an applicant who, having declared some rather unusual political and religious views, threatened to put a curse on the company if he was not given the job!

Having eliminated and politely replied to the obvious rejects, the remainder represent your 'possibles' and 'probables'. To make certain that these are dealt with as objectively as possible, the original person description can be used again. You can use either the profile itself or a shortened version as a check list against which to compare each application. Some recruiters find it helpful to attach a sheet of paper to each application listing the important requirements. A points score out of 5 is then jotted down against each requirement.

For example, let us suppose we are looking for an export office supervisor. The sheet of paper attached to each application might look something like this.

Score sheet for Mr Bloggs

Requirement	Score (out of 5)
Age range 30–50 years	5
Knowledge of French	5
Supervisory experience	0
Exporting experience	4
Micro-computer knowledge	2?
Formal qualifications	1
Available to work anti-social hours	5

The scores given will probably be rather subjective in some cases but this system is much more reliable than a general impression gained only from reading the letter or curriculum vitae. Some scores will either be 0 or 5. For example, someone is either within or outside the age range. However, you could decide that the nearer the applicant is to the average of the age range, or one of the extremes, the higher the score. Let us take a closer look at the scores for our potential export office supervisor.

Mr Bloggs scores high on age, being well within the range (let's suppose he is 39 years old). We have given him 5 for knowledge of French on the basis of a claim to spoken and written fluency. This can easily be confirmed so it is safe at this stage to accept what he says as correct.

Bloggs has 0 for supervising experience because he is a senior clerk at present and admits that he has no one under his supervision. This may be due to his personality, which previous employers may have judged unsuitable for a leadership position. This is something which can be explored at the interview stage and, if things go that far, with his previous employer. We must also consider the possibility that he, and other applicants, are looking for promotion and that he can be given supervisor training.

The score of 4 for exporting experience results from the number of years he has had in an exporting job. We reckoned that one point should be awarded for each year of relevant experience.

We have put a 2 followed by a question mark against Bloggs's computer knowledge score as he was rather vague about this in his letter. We recognise that this is not something which can be clearly stated in a relatively brief letter and is also something that we can check at the interview stage.

Formal qualifications are rated as 1 as he has no qualifications in exporting but he has two A levels. The A levels indicate a reasonable IQ and ability to learn. The top score of 5 for anti-social hours is due to his statement that he works such hours already and that this is not a problem.

The score sheet can now be considered for two purposes: to decide if we want to interview the applicant, and to identify subjects to concentrate on or clarify in the interview.

On the face of it, Mr Bloggs looks suitable for interviewing unless there are a number of other applicants who score better all round. In real life it is unlikely that anyone will fit the ideal profile and score top marks for every attribute. Even if someone did achieve such a score we might discard him at interview as the wrong personality type or even discover that he was lying.

If we do decide to interview Mr Bloggs a note can be made indicating the topics to concentrate on in discussion. If there are a number of other apparently better applicants we can always consider putting Bloggs on a reserve list – and send him a polite and friendly letter explaining that there will be a delay.

An alternative job?

While sifting through applications you may find that you can fill a second or even anticipated vacancy from among the applicants for the advertised job. For example, if Bloggs is not the preferred man for the exporting job he might be ideal in the translation section. Much time and money can be saved by considering good people (who are not wanted for a particular job) for another job which is going begging.

Application forms

Recruiters fall broadly into two camps. Some insist that an application form is essential, others regard them as a bureaucratic nonsense. The truth probably lies somewhere in between and whether or not you use them will depend on the demands of your particular situation. The arguments in favour of forms include the following claims:

- all applications will be written in the same format thus making it easier to read and compare them.
- application forms enforce provision of the information required.
- the completed form provides the basis of an employee record file.

  Opponents will argue that:

- if the advertisement is clear about the information required, worthwhile applicants will provide it in a letter or curriculum vitae. This makes a form unnecessary.
- application forms irritate and deter a percentage of applicants.
- more experienced and senior applicants regard a curriculum vitae as a better guide to their skills than even the best-designed form.
- application forms tend to ask for irrelevant information. This wastes time and in some cases can cause applicants to withdraw.
- a letter can tell you more than the mechanical answers to the mechanical questions provided on a form.
- a form limits the freedom of expression of the applicant, thus giving a distorted impression.
- forms create additional work for all concerned.
- application forms do not normally end up as the basis of an employee record. Employers frequently use some sort of record card (or cards) on to which data is laboriously copied from the application form and elsewhere.

  These are the pros and cons and each recruiter needs to make his own decision – in the light of his own circumstances. Small companies who recruit infrequently will probably manage very well without a form. So also will those organisations such as law firms, publishers, advertising agencies and public relations consultants who may regard the nature and quality of an applicant's letter as part of the selection process. However, if you decide to use a form it really must be properly designed.

Designing the application form

Examination of an actual *professionally designed* form in use in the United Kingdom revealed a great many failings. For instance, applicants are asked if they are legally eligible for employment in the UK. The number who would reply 'No, I am an illegal immigrant' must be very small indeed.

Other questions include:

> Do you have any physical condition which could limit your ability to perform the job . . . If so describe how you would be able to perform the job in spite of it.
> and Do you have a current driving licence? What relevance this has to the majority of jobs not involving driving is not clear.

In addition, the form asks:

> Have you ever been convicted of a criminal offence, other than a spent conviction under the Rehabilitation of Offenders Act 1974?

The words YES/NO are then added. Obviously former criminals are expected to cross out NO. However, a space 18 centimetres long is left in the box containing the question. As will be seen later, this wasted space could have been used elsewhere to good effect.

Later on, the applicant is asked, 'Have you previously worked for us? YES/NO. If yes, when?' The space provided for the dates of any previous employment measures 18 by 1.8 centimetres, whereas the actual space required is about a quarter of this amount.

The form goes on to ask for details of school, college and further education with examinations, courses and results. There is barely enough space for this and, if the applicant gained a double 1st at Oxford combined with an MBA at a business school, the fact that he obtained an O level in History at Slough Secondary Modern is likely to be irrelevant.

The penultimate section of the form provides completely inadequate spaces for some very important information – the applicant's employment history. The space in which he is expected to write details of work done in previous jobs measures 12 by 1.5 centimetres. The reason for leaving must be written in a space measuring 3 by 0.5 centimetres. This is barely enough to write one word in the block capitals required.

The space in which to write the salary received in previous jobs is less than half a centimetre square – just enough to write a single digit! In view of the wasted space in other parts of the form this particular nonsense could have been avoided.

The essential rules for a good application form are:

- only ask for information which is really needed. Details such as next of kin can be dealt with later, if at all.
- provide adequate space for the answers, taking into account what the applicant is expected to insert.
- avoid questions which may be regarded (however uncertainly) as discriminatory. Anything relating to race, religion, political interests and physical disabilities needs *very* careful consideration.
- give the applicant the option of writing in appropriate spaces 'see cv' if that will avoid him wasting his time. The form can have a notice printed on it reading, 'Please answer only those questions not already answered in your letter or cv.'
- place the questions in a logical sequence, e.g. name followed by address, and employment history in a separate section from personal details.

Taking up references

No references should be taken up at this stage – and *never* without the applicant's prior permission. (The matter of references will be dealt with in Chapter 5, page 70.)

Unemployed applicants

A study carried out by Cranfield School of Management indicated that sacked (and presumably also redundant) executives tended to be 'less conformist' and less politically shrewd than those who survive the organisational rat race. The study also suggested that they were on balance more energetic, imaginative and creative.

This strongly suggests that those recruiters who rule out unemployed applicants should think again. As Michael Dixon of the *Financial Times* jobs column wrote in January 1987, when describing the Cranfield study, 'The stupidity of imposing them [bans on unemployed people] has been several times shown by research.'

The fact that many recruiters will not consider unemployed people was shown in a 1987 report prepared by the Institute of Manpower Studies (IMS). The report showed that unemployed applicants are likely to be rejected in not less than 50 per cent of cases. This, it said, was due to a belief on the part of some employers that unemployed people lacked motivation, had lost the work habit and had lost the ability to do the job.

For these and other reasons it seems that a substantial number of unemployed people are screened out at an early stage of the selection process. It is significant, however, that in cases where unemployed applicants reached the interview stage their chances improved considerably. In an interview the applicants have the opportunity to explain *why* they are unemployed and demonstrate their motivation and positive attitude to work.

The IMS report also showed that employers' attitudes to the unemployed are favourably influenced by actual experience of recruiting them and working with them.

The smart employer, faced with an application from an unemployed person, will take the view that, given the necessary experience and skills, the unemployed applicant may in practice turn out to be a more dedicated employee. Being unemployed is a thoroughly nasty experience – few people would risk going through it again because of bad work or lack of effort.

Some unemployed people may require training but this does not always present an obstacle as the following example shows. A catering company, finding it impossible to recruit the trained staff needed for expanding business, decided deliberately to recruit from the unemployed. A total of about 70 unemployed people were taken on and put through a training programme to turn them into the operatives needed.

Of course this costs money. But, it is useful to ask yourself whether the cost of training is likely to be greater then the cost of repeated advertising. If so, how much greater? And will the cost be balanced (or more than balanced) by the additional income generated by new business – business which would not be possible without the new staff?

It is not difficult to imagine situations where the development of a business is curtailed by a lack of staff. Indeed, regular complaints of skilled staff shortages are to be found in most European countries. If, say, a new contract can be accepted as a result of training unemployed people then the problem could be solved.

In addition, even when a ready-trained person is taken on there is often an element of re-training to familiarise the newcomer with company standards, procedures, policies and so on. One distinct advantage of training someone from scratch is that *your* company standards and ways of doing things can be more readily instilled. You will know how and what the newcomer has been taught and can thus be more certain of how he will deal with customers, for example.

Application dos and don'ts

- **don't** make it difficult for people to apply for your job. **Do** make the application procedure friendly, simple and easy.

- **do** treat applicants with courtesy and respect. **Do** keep them informed and keep delays to a minimum.

- **do** analyse applications methodically using a check list based on the person description and avoiding subjectivity as much as possible.

- **do** provide likely candidates with a full job description and plenty of information about your company before they attend for interview.

- **do** consider good people, to whom you cannot offer the job, for other vacancies you may have or expect to have.

- if you must use an application form, **do** make it logical and user-friendly.

- **don't** automatically reject unemployed or disabled applicants.

- **do** consider deliberately taking on and training unemployed people if you are unable to find the trained people you have been looking for.

5

INTERVIEWING AND OTHER SELECTION METHODS

WRITING in *The Times* in November 1987, William Isbister, an occupational psychologist with many years of selection experience, said of selection methods:

> . . . one needs to be reminded that any technique which is used is only as good as the person who uses it. My belief is that there have been no big advances and that the general standard of picking people throughout occupational and public life remains abysmally low, and is too often disgraceful.

Talking about 'new' techniques (psychometric testing and the like), Isbister made the following comment – one which will be echoed by many managers who are not among the ranks of those selling the 'new' techniques for a fat fee:

> The new techniques are deceptive, having the appearance of some validity . . . and hence hold the promise of a false dawn. There is nought for the comfort of line managers, who throughout my working lifetime have ached for the Holy Grail . . .

This all sounds pretty depressing. Here we have an experienced professional telling us that standards of selection are abysmal and that the 'new' techniques on offer are suspect. Yes, he is right but all is not lost. It *is* possible to make a decent job of staff selection (although there will always be some failures of course).

Interviewing

Let us review what has been done so far, in order to put the interview in context. Firstly, you have taken a lot of trouble over describing the job to be done. Secondly, you have worked out the type of person you are looking for, both in ideal and in minimum terms. Thirdly, you have received some applications from which the 'closest fit' people have been sifted by a reasonably objective process.

If all this preliminary work has been done carefully then the interview has only three purposes:

- to confirm that the information provided by the applicant is the truth and the whole truth
- to make a judgement as to whether or not the applicant has the personality for the job and will 'fit in'
- to decide which applicant – if there are two or more – fits the person description most closely, both in personality and skills.

The second of these requirements is the most difficult since judgements tend to be subjective and influenced by preconceived notions about people. There are, however, some easy ways to reduce the chances of error and these will be explained later in this chapter (page 69).

The first requirement, confirming the information already provided, can be done in three ways: by questioning and listening, by testing and by taking up references. The references, although not part of the interview itself, can follow closely after it and form part of the whole process of selection. (These are discussed in more detail later on in this chapter, page 70.)

The purpose of the interview

The purpose, you may say, is obvious – to find a suitable person to fill the vacancy. Of course this is correct but it can be approached in one of two ways. According to a study of British employers carried out by the Institute of Manpower Studies in 1988 the majority of recruiters are more concerned with weeding out the *wrong* person than identifying the *right* one. The IMS stated:

> Most of the recruitment and selection which goes on in the United Kingdom organisations relies on the ability of person-nel and line managers to disqualify inappropriate candidates.

The report also suggests that much the same situation can be found in other countries including Australia, Canada and the USA.

Clearly the recruiter's attitude will have a marked effect on the way the selection process is applied and, possibly, on the quality of the results. There is a vast difference between 'We cannot find any faults in Miss Bloggs so we have offered her the job' and 'Miss Bloggs was seen to have the abilities we are looking for and potential for the future.'

It is therefore important to adopt a positive attitude, especially when approaching the interview stage. None of the selection stages should be treated as a fault-finding expedition. They should all be treated as a search for gold dust. The applicant with most 'gold dust' is likely to be a better employee than the one with fewest faults, although sometimes both features will be found in the same person.

Apart from a negative attitude, there are many other destructive approaches to interviewing. Some people treat it as an adversarial process akin to a cross-examination in a criminal court. Others use the interview as an opportunity to show off ('I'm a very important manager round here, young fellow'). The very worst interviewers exercise their sadistic tendencies by bullying the applicant with aggressive questions. This is done in the guise of 'finding out what he is made of'.

None of these approaches deserves to be considered as interviewing techniques. The interview should be a relaxed, friendly and constructive exchange of information in which two people explore their suitability for each other in an employer/employee relationship. And the success of such an exchange will be significantly influenced by what precedes it.

Before the interview

There is quite a bit of preparation and administration to be done before the interview. And these preliminaries must not be regarded as boring or something to be glossed over. They form an *essential* part of successful selection. To set the right atmosphere you should first arrange the time and the place of the meeting to suit the applicant as far as possible. It is also very important to send the applicant clear instructions on how to get to the factory or office. These should be fairly detailed and include such information as:

- suggested travel routes
- bus route numbers

- nearest rail station
- street map
- which building to go to (if there is more than one)
- which entrance to use (if there is more than one)
- which floor of the building
- and the name of the person to ask for.

Warn the applicant if the interview is likely to be lengthy *and* if any tests will be involved. You also need to ensure that you have allowed yourself ample time. A minimum of 40 minutes should be required for a junior and an hour or more for managerial and other more senior staff.

Finally, make sure that you have a suitable room available for the interview. Ideally the room will be quite private (no glass panels through which curious people can stare) and will be clean, tidy and comfortable. Preferably there will be no telephone in the room. (There is nothing more irritating or discourteous to the applicant than breaking off an interview to take a telephone call.) The interview room should be a friendly place with no desk between the interviewer and applicant. Desks are not only physical barriers, they are psychological ones too. Two comfortable chairs placed in front of a small, low, round table is an arrangement which is far more likely to encourage good communication.

These preparatory measures will help to get things going along the right lines. They will, for example, help to avoid the applicant getting lost, arriving late and performing badly due to sheer embarrassment. This, in turn, will help you keep to a timetable – vital if you have a number of people to see on the same day.

When the applicant arrives

If all goes well the applicant will arrive on time and be fairly relaxed. You should have ensured that the receptionist is aware that he is coming and, armed with his name, can give a polite and friendly welcome.

While waiting for the interview the applicant should be made 'comfortable'. He should be given the opportunity to use a lavatory and be offered coffee, tea or other refreshment. The applicant may well have travelled for some distance and may also be nervous (perhaps even afraid to ask to use a lavatory). Applicants who are thirsty or bursting to go to the lavatory will not interview as well as they otherwise would and you might reject the best person for the job as a result.

Don't keep the applicant waiting too long. Horror stories abound of applicants hanging about while the interviewer deals with an 'urgent' telephone call or is 'unavoidably delayed'. Some of these tales are undoubtedly exaggerated but one true story concerns Julia, a young graduate applying for her first job. Julia arrived on time, was kept waiting for about half an hour and was then told by the personnel manager that there would be a further delay *while he went for lunch.*

Not only is this sort of behaviour grossly discourteous, it is also unfair and unprofessional. It is unfair because it offends and worries the applicant, who may have no time to spare. Many people applying for jobs have taken time off from an existing job and may have some very difficult explaining to do if they are away too long. It is also unprofessional because it makes a successful interview less likely and in many cases could cause the applicant to change his mind about working for the company concerned. It will also prolong the period of stress which, to a greater or lesser extent, all applicants suffer while waiting. The greater the stress the less likely it is that the applicant will give an accurate impression of himself.

All applicants are important to the company, have cost money to find and should be treated accordingly. However if you follow the above advice the scene will be correctly set and there will be a friendly, creative atmosphere. The interview itself comes next.

Opening the interview

The interviewer will have made some further preparations including:

- reading the applicant's details. This should be done just before the interview so that the facts are fresh in your mind. The applicant will expect you to be familiar with the information he has given you and his answers to questions will be influenced by this. For example, if he has mentioned his special training in telex operating in his application letter he may not refer to it again when asked if he has any special skills to offer.
- preparing a check list of questions, including any queries raised by comparing the applicant with the person description (as described in Chapter 4).

- preparing the answers to questions which the applicant may ask on such topics as salary, pension scheme, working hours, trade union membership, holiday entitlement, training schemes and, of course, details of the work to be done.
- having a full job description and an organisation chart with which to explain the job and its relationship to other jobs in the company.

Armed with all this information, the first priority is to maintain the relaxed atmosphere. This can be done by opening the interview with a friendly greeting and a few words on some neutral subject. 'Did you have any trouble finding us?' or some similar question will suffice, combined perhaps with some small talk about local traffic conditions, parking problems or whatever. This is *not* a waste of time as it can help to settle both people down and will encourage a more satisfactory flow of information later.

Of course that is what the interview is all about – a flow of information. And this flow can start with a careful explanation of the job to be done and its content. This need not be lengthy but should be sufficient to ensure that the applicant has a clear and accurate picture of what is required. Without a clear understanding the applicant cannot be expected to give wholly sensible and intelligible answers to later questions. Talking at cross-purposes is no more rare in job interviews than in any other form of oral communication, unless care is taken to avoid it.

Following the explanation of the job and an opportunity for the applicant to ask any clarifying questions, the 'investigation' stage of the interview can begin.

The investigational stage

Questions can be a very powerful tool. Using questions the skilled interviewer can control the conversation, introduce or re-introduce subjects and find out the facts. This is not as difficult as it might seem and does not require training in interrogation techniques! A combination of common sense and 'open' questions are all that is needed. An open question is one which demands more than a yes or no answer. The following examples illustrate ways in which such questions may be used. Firstly, you could use them to discuss the applicant's likes and dislikes and attitudes to superiors or colleagues:

'What do you most like about your present job?'

'What do you most dislike about your present job?'

'What sort of person do you most like working for?'

Note that if the question 'Why?' is used after each answer a great deal more can be discovered.

Open questions can also be used to test the applicant's willingness to learn new skills:

'Which subjects do you think you should learn more about in order to improve your abilities?'

'Which business subjects have you most enjoyed learning since you left school?'

'What made you decide to take a course in book-keeping?'

Bearing in mind the need to look for 'gold dust', questions can be asked to reveal strengths and abilities relevant to the job:

'What statistical techniques do you find most helpful in quality control work?'

'How do you see us using your sales experience in organising our publicity campaign?'

'In what ways can your knowledge of motor mechanics be used in this job?'

Of course, you could ask more direct questions but these would indicate the 'right answer' and that is what you might get. For example:

'Do you get on with your boss?'
Right answer: 'Yes'

'Are you prepared to learn more about stock control?'
Right answer: 'Yes'

Answers such as these merely leave you wondering whether you can believe them or not.

You must *listen to* the answers carefully. What is *not* said can be equally revealing and can demand a further open question to probe further. It is also important to give the applicant time to consider his answer before replying. Pressurising the applicant by showing impatience will inhibit clear thinking on his part and may result in misleading answers. Similarly, answers should not be interrupted as this can confuse the applicant and create stress.

Keep in mind that you are trying to build up a picture of the person you are listening to. This picture should have no significant holes in it and further searching questions may be necessary to fill in the empty spaces. Many questions will occur to you as you go along – however carefully the preparation and anticipation was done. For example, you may have a sudden doubt as to whether or not the applicant works well in a team. If so, a couple of relevant open questions may be needed. For example:

'What kind of holidays do you prefer?'
(Walking alone in the mountains is quite different from joining a group of friends for a week in a noisy resort.)

'What kind of sports do you most enjoy?'
(Team games suggest one thing, squash or swimming alone another.)

Allowing for the fact that most people enjoy some time to themselves (e.g. reading or gardening), the answer can indicate what sort of relationships the applicant has with other people. However, do avoid the mistake of warming to a person whose interests happen to be the same as your own and assuming that he must be the right type for the job. Such a conclusion can be very wrong.

The reverse should also be avoided. One applicant for a job was turned down by a senior manager to the surprise of an impressed personnel officer.

'I thought he was an excellent candidate,' said the personnel officer.

'I thought he was boring,' said the manager. 'He likes astronomy – I can't think of anything I like less.'

Some interviewers find it helpful to ask questions about the applicant's private and working life in three stages – the past, the present and the future. This method provides a framework which helps to prevent the questions and the answers becoming haphazard.

Under 'past', questions can be asked about:
- previous jobs
- achievements at work
- achievements outside work
- and disappointments.

The 'present' group of questions could cover:
- attitudes, likes and dislikes
- views on current affairs
- why a change of job is being contemplated
- and interests.

The 'future' might be probed by asking about:
- aspirations
- ambitions
- and plans.

Questions on some or all of these subjects will help to create a picture of the *person* now, his past record and how he sees his future.

'Clever' questions

There are some very rare jobs which require unusual characteristics in the people who do them. For jobs such as those of an SAS trooper or an astronaut it may be necessary to subject candidates to a style of questioning which is wholly unsuitable for the vast majority of people. Unfortunately some interviewers feel that they should use such questions and amply demonstrate their ignorance in doing so.

Examples of 'clever' questions taken from real life business interviews are:

'What do you dislike about me?'

'When did you last lose your temper and why?'

'What is your favourite colour?'

'Why do you wear a beard?'

Questions of this type, when devised by a trained psychologist, *may* be an appropriate way to probe into the depths of someone's personality if required. They should be avoided in all normal interviews because they could result in the applicant feeling confused, frightened, embarrassed, or even insulted.

In addition, unless the interviewer is a specialist psychologist, it is unlikely that he will be able to evaluate the answer in any meaningful way. I was once asked which was my favourite colour. I answered, 'None, I am colour blind.' What the interviewer made of my response was not revealed.

Note-taking

It is difficult, when paying close attention to what the applicant is saying, to make copious notes. However, unless the interviewer's memory is particularly good a few 'shorthand' jottings should be made on important points. Some interviewers find it useful to compile a check list of questions with tick boxes in which they can quickly indicate their degree of satisfaction with the answer.

Whatever brief notes are taken during the interview it is important to make more comprehensive notes *immediately* afterwards. Time should be allowed for this and it should be regarded as an essential part of the interview process. It is not good enough to write up an assessment 'when things are less busy' or at night when you are tired and thinking less clearly.

Closing the interview

Towards the end of the interview both you and the applicant will have formed at least a provisional view on whether or not it is worth pursuing matters any further. The applicant may have some unspoken doubts or reservations about his suitability for the job or some aspect of it. The interviewer should encourage the applicant to express any such doubts. This will serve the useful dual purpose of correcting any false impressions (on either side) and enabling the applicant to assist you in making a decision.

The interviewer can also express any doubts he has, to achieve the same result. It is not at all unusual for an interviewer to doubt, say, the applicant's ability to perform a certain task. If the doubt is expressed the applicant may be prompted to come out with hitherto unmentioned experience which removes the doubt and would otherwise have remained unmentioned. This is another aspect of looking for 'gold dust'.

By now the applicant will also have formed impressions of the interviewer and the company. The closing stage of the interview is the last opportunity to ensure that the impression you have made is good – and that the applicant has been dealt with fairly and efficiently. The following steps are suggested:

- ask the applicant if there are any more questions he wishes to ask.
- thank him for coming to see you and give some indication of how soon you will be in touch with him again. Be careful not to

imply that the candidate has the job if you are as yet undecided. You do not want to cause unnecessary disappointment.

- offer travel expenses if they have been incurred. (Some companies will not pay applicants' travel expenses 'as a matter of principle'. If you want to confirm that your company is mean and will give niggardly pay rises, refusing to pay expenses is a first-class way to go about it.

- see the applicant off the premises with a friendly smile and a handshake. Even if you have already decided that the applicant is someone you do not want there is no mileage in making them dislike you or your company.

The follow-up

There is still quite a lot of hard work to be done after the interview is over. To some recruiters the post-interview stage is the hardest of all – because an important decision may be required.

A number of scenarios may have developed. Firstly, the applicant may be clearly unsuitable. If so, there is no reason why he should not have been told this diplomatically at the end of the interview, with a convincing explanation of the reason why. This would at least have left him knowing where he stood without the agony of waiting for the postman to deliver your rejection letter. Whether or not the applicant was told on the spot a polite and friendly letter should be promptly sent confirming the decision and thanking him for his interest.

One very large British company does not do this. They merely ignore any applicants they do not want – thereby creating an ever-growing army of people who hold them in contempt. It is interesting to note that this company has tried hard to recruit certain specialists. The word has gone round and many of these specialists have chosen to ignore them and apply to their competitors instead.

Another possibility is that the applicant is suitable but not the best of a shortlist. In such cases a 'hold' letter is needed while the preferred applicant makes up his mind. This precaution should not be neglected as it can be costly to find that the preferred applicant has turned you down – when you have turned down a suitable reserve candidate.

If the applicant is suitable *and* the best of the shortlist you should send a prompt offer letter as soon as the decision is made. A friendly touch which encourages a prompt reply (you are now the one who is waiting for the postman) is the enclosure of a stamped addressed envelope.

Alternatively, one or more applicants may appear to be suitable but a further interview is needed before a final decision can be made. This situation often arises as a result of initial 'screening' interviews being carried out by whoever is responsible for personnel matters. The appropriate supervisor or manager then needs to see the likely applicants.

Delays can be avoided if managers see promising applicants immediately after the first interview, or are present at it themselves. However this is not always possible if, say, four people are being interviewed. Asking the first to hang about until the others have been seen is likely to be an unreasonable request.

In any event, the supervisor or manager must see the preferred person or people since they will be responsible for them and their work. Furthermore, the manager should be the person best placed to decide whether the applicant will fit in. Any necessary second interview should be arranged without delay.

Finally, we have the applicant who is not suitable but could be considered for an alternative post. Ideally, this possibility will be put to him before the interview ends so that some discussion on it can take place there and then. If this is not possible a letter suggesting the alternative job should be sent promptly.

Analysis and comparisons

Fairly quick decisions can sometimes be made but in most cases time will be needed to reach a conclusion. The first task is to compare the applicant with the original person description. It is most unlikely that any applicant will fit precisely but you need some objective way to see how close he comes. A common method is to award a point score against the attributes required, as described in Chapter 4, page 50.

The second stage is comparing the applicant with an existing employee who does the job well. This will again be subjective to some extent but it is normally a useful exercise – if only to focus the mind on what attributes really do matter.

Thirdly, you need to compare one applicant with another. Looking at the points scored by each candidate for each of the attributes helps to eliminate 'general' impressions which are influenced by a failure to remember items of detail. It is by no means easy to remember every candidate in relation to each attribute, and using the points score is more reliable.

In any of these methods there is a danger to be avoided – prejudice. All human beings are prejudiced in some way and there are many more prejudices than the traditional ones of sex, race and religion. From infancy, everyone is subject to conditioning which starts with the influence of parents, extends through friends, teachers, work colleagues and others, to the media.

The result is that, whether consciously or not, people we meet are judged on a whole range of criteria such as accent, dress, height, weight, voice, social background, type of education and interests. From time to time one comes across some quite bizarre prejudices, such as the man who mistrusted men who wore bow ties or the administration director who positively disliked people who walked slowly!

Everyone is prone to form mental stereotypes – perhaps as a result of one event in their lives – and the danger is that the stereotyping is allowed to influence judgements in an irrational way. This phenomenon can be entertainingly demonstrated by playing a game with a few people chosen for their common sense and balanced personalities. The game is played as follows:

> Divide the people into pairs. Give both people in a pair the same head and shoulders photograph of someone dressed in a 'neutral' fashion. Tell one of them that the photograph is of a second-hand car salesman and the other that the person is a bank manager.
>
> Then ask each person to describe, based on appearance, the characteristics of the person in the photograph.

The responses can be most revealing and often hilarious. In one such test the 'car salesman' was described as shifty – because his eyes were close together. The 'bank manager' was described as having integrity – because his eyes were wide apart. Not only were the beliefs about the *profession* of the subject strong enough to determine his characteristics, they were also strong enough to create wholly different perceptions of visible physical characteristics. In fact the man in the picture was an entomologist. The same test can be repeated with more pairs of people and other alternative professions such as: a racing driver and a missionary, an estate agent and a librarian, a union leader and a tax inspector.

The shrewd interviewer will admit to himself (it is not necessary to bare the soul to others) that he has prejudices. He will then do everything possible to set them aside when making judgements on job applicants. Admitting to the prejudice is the hardest part but, once achieved, makes setting it aside much easier.

References

Taking up references is an essential part of the follow-up process. However, most written references are a waste of time and many referees will not be entirely honest on paper. Any seriously adverse comments could result in a legal action – even if the law regards a reference as 'privileged'. A telephone call to the referee can be much more revealing and allows questions to be put to confirm what the applicant has claimed. The telephone call should also be used to look for the 'gold dust'. Some useful questions to ask on the telephone are:

'Would you take the applicant back into your company? If not, why not?'

'What, in your view, are the applicant's strong points?'

'What are his weak points?'

and, having briefly described the job you are trying to fill,

'How well do you think the applicant would fit such a job?'

It is very important *not* to take up references without the applicant's prior knowledge and consent. An applicant for a job with a major European airline was interviewed and told that he would be called for interview again. He was told that no references would be taken up until after the second interview and then only with his knowledge and if satisfactory references were all that stood between him and the job.

Two days later the applicant's boss angrily demanded to know why he was applying for another job. The boss made it clear that he regarded this action as a sign of disloyalty and that it would be taken into account in future. The applicant telephoned the airline and asked why a reference had been asked for without his agreement. The answer was simple – it was company policy. Needless to say the applicant withdrew, wondering what other company policies he might fall foul of if he joined the airline.

Other kinds of interview

There are, in addition to the commonly used one-to-one interview, a number of alternatives which should be considered.

The panel interview

In this alternative the candidate sits opposite a panel of perhaps four people who normally face him across a long table. Some panels comprise as many as 10 people. The more people, the more frightening they can be to an immature applicant.

The argument in favour of panels has it that the combined wisdom of a number of people is more likely to achieve a successful outcome than one person. There is no evidence that this is true. Possibly the only advantage is in avoiding a lengthy series of one-to-one sessions in cases where a lot of people insist on seeing the applicant and voicing an opinion.

In the case of business partnerships if, as infrequently happens, an outsider is being brought into the partnership, there may be some value in this. Normally, however, additions to partnerships are by invitation to existing employees or well-known outsiders. Otherwise the panel interview is perhaps best left to such bodies as town or county councillors and other politicians who are reluctant to keep out of anything.

The argument against panels, apart from their inhibiting effect on nervous applicants, is that they multiply the weaknesses and defects of one-to-one interviewing. There is certainly anecdotal evidence that any prejudice present in the more influential panel members will be increased by the opportunity to demonstrate it to the others.

The interview series

The safety in numbers principle is sometimes applied by arranging a lengthy series of interviews. As many as five or six interviewers will see the applicant, either one immediately after the other, or spread over a number of days. The process is an exhausting one for the applicant and might well drive away potentially good people who could justifiably ask how long the company needs to make up its mind.

The advantage, if there is one, is probably more political than anything else. One senior executive always insists on his immediate colleagues joining in the interviewing sessions so that if the person selected turns out to be a disappointment they will share the blame! Clearly there is some value in a second or even a third opinion but it is unlikely that much will be gained by extending the process any further.

The social interview

This method is not often used but is an excellent way to check whether the applicant is likely to fit in – the most difficult part of selection. The idea is the simple one of placing the applicant in an informal and friendly social scene along with those who would be his closest colleagues. The putative colleagues will soon form a judgement of the applicant's compatibility – or lack of it.

This approach does *not* include the formal lunch on company premises. This latter method, much favoured by financial institutions in London, New York, Frankfurt and other financial centres, is only suitable for applicants for high-level jobs and has marginal value in assessing compatibility. Such occasions tend to be too stiff and formal for any reliable impression to be formed. Everyone at such meetings knows what can be said or talked about in advance and it is more in the nature of a social ritual than anything else.

However an invitation to meet potential future colleagues over a beer at a pub or over a meal in an informal restaurant can be very useful. I have used this approach on a number of occasions – and always with good results. Whenever the team have liked an applicant he has always been a successful choice. Naturally such meetings start somewhat stiffly but as time passes barriers break down. The applicant who fits in to the work environment is also the one who fits into the social environment and this becomes apparent when minor confidences gradually begin to be shared, jokes exchanged and general rapport developed.

The applicant who is approved of by the team will also have the support of colleagues when he starts work. This enhances the chance of success and almost guarantees an absence of jealousies, petty prejudices and the like. As one former colleague remarked about an applicant, 'She likes a drink and a good laugh so she must be OK.' Although this was a partly facetious remark it is on such judgements that successful teamwork can depend.

Alternatives to interviewing

It is a sad fact of life that no one has yet discovered a wholly successful selection method. The traditional interview – even when most carefully applied – can result in failure. For many years business people and others (such as governments, police forces and the military in every industrialised country) have searched for a really reliable method. Not infrequently, someone claims to have found the answer and, of course, this is offered to the world at large for a substantial fee. There are dozens of 'psychological' tests, 'structural' methods and goodness knows what else on offer. There is even one called a 'holistic' system.

The argument in favour of these various evaluation techniques is that they are not subject to prejudice, gut instinct, hunches and other subjective influences. It is interesting to set this claim against some comments made by Chris Lewis, principal lecturer at North-East London Polytechnic. According to *Personnel Management* (November 1988), Lewis told a conference on testing that psychological testing stands up well against other techniques such as the interview, but it has just as much potential for misuse:

> Although a test in itself might be reliable, the user of that test still held considerable power . . . recruiters could decide exactly who they were going to test and, if they did discriminate in the selection process . . . they could use tests to back up the decision.

It has also been argued that the 'scientific' techniques achieve better results in practice, whatever the reason may be. There is limited evidence to support such claims and since they are mainly put forward by the people who sell the systems it is wise to adopt a cautious approach. Then again, it would not be sensible to ignore them, as any means of raising success levels is important to the success and profitability of the business seeking good staff.

It is only fair to point out that psychological tests have had *some* support from independent sources. The Institute of Manpower Studies report referred to earlier in this chapter gave them some credibility, at least by saying that they were a little more dependable than interviews.

The methods which follow are the more commonly used ones – excluding astrology, graphology and phrenology – all of which have been recommended at some time or other and will no doubt continue to be.

Intelligence, aptitude and IQ tests

Most of these tests measure intelligence of a narrow kind. Based on questions which use mathematics or word reasoning, in a 'symbolic' way, they test the person's ability to manipulate data. The theory is that high-scoring people will have a sufficient level of intelligence to be successful at various jobs. The available evidence does not suggest any great success using such tests and much depends on the particular type of test used.

As part of an experiment, I once took three tests designed to assess aptitude for computer programming. One of the tests, designed by a French company, used a mixture of mathematical questions, word reasoning and diagrams. The others were respectively orientated to word reasoning and mathematical reasoning. The results of the tests, all taken on the same day, were remarkable. The French test suggested average ability. The word reasoning suggested very high ability and the mathematical test resulted in a score so low as to be disastrous.

From time to time, a variation or development of a traditional test emerges. One of them starts with a tape recording of the applicant in conversation. The recording is analysed to see how the applicant uses words. And the result is then compared with the way in which words are used by people who are already successful in the work in question. This approach has the obvious merit of comparing one of the applicant's attributes with an attribute of someone known to be successful. Time will tell whether the method offers any clear advantages over its predecessors or has any real validity at all.

Assessment centre testing

Although often described as a 'new' technique, the assessment centre has a long history. At such centres applicants are subjected to a variety of trials, including presentations, leadership exercises, negotiating sessions and group discussions. The theory is that over a period of perhaps two or three days the examiners will spot the strengths and weaknesses of the individuals taking part and be able to sort the sheep from the goats. This method has been used for several decades by the military in many countries to select suitable candidates for officer training.

A number of large international corporations have also used

assessment centres for many years, though there is no clear evidence that they work especially well. The former training director of a major international bank pointed out two weaknesses in this form of testing. Firstly, the fluent talker tends to do well when compared with less extrovert people. Slick talking may disguise weaknesses. And secondly, the examiners are likely to be influenced by their personal likes and dislikes.

Exactly the same criticism can be made of interviewing, and in both cases success or failure will depend on the ability and common sense of the examiner or interviewer.

Psychometric tests

Like IQ tests, these comprise a series of questions. Designed by psychologists, the questions are intended to assess a range of attributes such as tenacity, ability to work with others, ambition, motivation, commitment and so on.

It could be argued that the reliability of psychometric tests depends wholly on the psychologists getting the questions (and the answers) right in the first place. This means that for any particular job or type of work they will need to be sure of what the 'right' answer is to a particular question – or what a particular answer means. Given that human beings are infinitely varied and that words have different shades of meaning for different people, it is not easy to place a great deal of faith in the psychologists – who are also human – getting it right.

Psychometric tests might be more convincing if they could be designed specifically for each individual taking them. However if that much were known about someone the test would probably not be necessary! Once again, there is no clear evidence that these tests are especially reliable.

Word surveys

This is a self-evaluation technique examining the applicants choice of words which is said to produce an accurate picture of an applicant's temperament – and thus a clear indication of how he will handle the job in question. Since temperament cannot be the only deciding factor it would seem that word surveys are unlikely to be the whole answer. A word survey test may however be helpful in coming to a decision if doubts about temperament are all that remains to be cleared up.

The scored life history method

Using what amounts to a long and very detailed application form, the answers to various questions relating to the applicant's past are each given a score (out of a certain number of points). Undoubtedly, past performance and influences will be some guide to a person's abilities but not necessarily a full or accurate guide. It is very hard to predict how a person will react when subjected to new influences, pressures and a different environment. This is one reason why people can perform well in one company and badly in another.

Structured interviews

This is a system of interviewing in which sets of questions must be put to the applicant in a particular and unvarying way. There is a 'right' answer to each question which, one authority stated, could be discovered in advance by reading the appropriate books.

These then are just some of the alternatives or supplements to the normal interview. They should be used with great care and only by people who really understand them. Claims of great success should be treated with caution and evidence seen before paying for either a testing package or an 'expert' to help you.

It is likely that careful thought and preparation, followed by an interview and yet more careful thought, will yield as high a level of success as can reasonably be expected. Companies who can afford it might use psychological tests or whatever as an experiment to compare with interviewing – or as part of the pre-interview preparation. A psychological test might point to subjects that need probing during the interview and, to this extent, could be helpful.

However you choose to conduct the interview, it is undoubtedly true that good induction and subsequent skilled management of the individual is *at least* as important in deciding whether you end up with a good employee or a bad one.

The contract of employment

Once you have offered the job to the best candidate you must agree on the terms of employment. These cover salary, working hours, holiday entitlement, pension and sickness schemes, etc. Every newcomer is entitled to a contract of employment and there are legal provisions which provide for the content of that contract and the terms which must be described. Drawing up a contract of employment is a legal area, and you have got to get it right. It is unwise to devise a contract or a letter of agreement (which amounts to the same thing as a contract) without first obtaining professional advice as to the minimum content and the precise wording.

Advice can be obtained either from a firm of solicitors specialising in employment law or from the Small Firms Service, ACAS or the Industrial Society.

Interviewing and selection dos and don'ts

- **don't** imagine that any selection method is perfect.
- **do** remember the primary purposes of an interview:
  - to confirm what is true
  - to form a 'fit-in' judgement
  - to look for 'gold dust', not faults
  - and to choose between applicants.
- **don't** treat interviewing as an adversarial process, or as an opportunity to show off.
- **do** prepare for the interview carefully with the applicant in mind. **Don't** neglect any precaution which will make the occasion a relaxed and constructive one for both parties.
- **do** remember that the applicant is a VIP. **Don't** make an enemy of him.
- **do** frame interview questions in an 'open' style to encourage the applicant to talk. **Don't** stop listening. **Don't** interrupt.
- **do** take brief notes and write them up more fully immediately after the interview.

77

- **don't** use 'clever' psychological questions unless they are truly appropriate *and* you have the know-how to interpret and evaluate the answers accurately.

- **do** check that there are no misunderstandings or false impressions on either side before the interview ends.

- **do** close the interview pleasantly and continue to treat the applicant as a VIP even if you are not intending to make him an offer.

- **don't** delay the follow-up. If you have definitely decided one way or another tell the applicant promptly. Otherwise keep the applicant informed.

- **do** take care with series interviews, panels and the like. They can put off good candidates if they are not sensitively organised.

- **do** take up references – with prior agreement and by telephone.

- **do** try to avoid allowing prejudices to cloud your judgement. **Don't** imagine that you have no prejudices – we all have them.

- **do** consider using the 'social interview' as a means to test whether a candidate 'fits in'.

- **do** be wary of special tests and 'new' systems which claim to select objectively and with great accuracy. Be sure that you know how reliable they are before spending money on them.

6

GETTING THEM STARTED

THE experience of starting a new job provides a rich fund of fascinating and horrifying tales. One young woman, commenting rather bitterly on her first few days in a new job, said:

> This was my first job as a secretary and I was looking forward to it. She [a member of the personnel department] took me to the underwriting department but my boss was not there. I spent the first three days with no work to do and no one took much notice of me as they were all too busy. My boss turned up on the fourth day but didn't speak to me until after lunch. He gave me some work at about 5 p.m. and told me I would have to work late . . .

By contrast, a systems analyst commented very differently on his first few days:

> My boss spent about an hour with me on my first morning before introducing me to the other people in the department. He gave me a copy of my job description and a list of objectives. I had never been given objectives before and it was nice to know what was expected of me. We [the systems analysts] all had lunch together which was nice and after lunch the boss discussed the objectives with me. The next day I was given my first assignment and one of the other guys was appointed to help me out with any problems in getting started . . .

The first few days in a new job can be a 'make or break' time, especially for young inexperienced people. The first impression often decides whether an employee will be happy and enthusiastic and whether or not he will stay with the company.

The first and simplest requirement is to make the newcomer

feel welcome as soon as he arrives. You will probably have spent time and money to find the new recruit and you will have had work waiting to be done. If such is the case you should be pleased and relieved to see him walk through the door. Showing your pleasure will be enormously encouraging to the new employee who will almost certainly feel apprehensive at the very least.

It is a useful exercise to think back over the years and try to remember your own experiences when starting a new job. Did you feel:

Worried?
Frightened?
Lonely?
That you didn't belong?
Uncertain about what you were expected to do?
Unsure who was who?
Unsure who your boss was?
That you didn't know where things were?
That you didn't understand the purpose of the work?
Confused by the jargon?
Uncertain about the company rules?
Discouraged?
Sorry that you had ever taken the job?
Angry about your treatment?
Misled by the interview?

If you suffered any experiences of this sort then someone let you and the company down.

The fact is that all these counter-productive situations can be avoided by a little thought, pre-planning and common sense.

Induction schemes

Company induction schemes – type A

Many companies have an employee induction scheme which, although well intended, is not nearly good enough. This is the type A scheme in which the employee is greeted rather formally and given a pile of documents explaining the pension scheme, car parking rules, codes of conduct ('Any employee found to be drunk on the premises will be instantly dismissed'), etc.

The employee is then conducted to his workplace and handed over to a busy boss who delegates the job of looking after the newcomer to a harassed subordinate (who probably did not know that the recruit was coming). Now regarded as adequately looked after, the newcomer is left to struggle along as best he can.

Such schemes are common in large manufacturing companies who seem to 'process' new employees as if they were machine parts moving down a production line. The same process can also be found in small companies which may not have a formal induction scheme at all but treat their new recruits in the same way. The result is that the newcomer begins to lose confidence, feels worried and resentful, and quite often leaves fairly rapidly.

Company induction schemes – type B

Type B schemes are designed around *the employee* and are constructed as much from the viewpoint of the individual as that of the company. In such schemes the employee is welcomed with a smile and a warm greeting. The first few hours are devoted to making the recruit feel 'comfortable' and may include introductions (not too many at first), directions to the loos, where to get a cup of coffee, an explanation of who's who, and so on.

At an early stage (preferably before the end of the first week), the recruit is taken through a well-presented explanation of the company culture (e.g. its ethical standards), history, products, structure and anything else which will help him find his feet. *All* recruits, whatever their level in the hierarchy, age or job, will receive the same presentation.

The newcomer is offered and given regular support and help to do the work required. This can range from ad hoc advice to formal and methodical training. He is given the opportunity to raise any difficulties he may have, and these are dealt with quickly and sympathetically. This induction process is continued into the first week, month, etc, with no sudden 'now you're on your own' break.

Setting up a new recruit programme

If your company wishes to set up its own new recruit programme it can be conveniently organised around a series of checklists. The checklists will deal with the first day, the first week and so on. They will then be divided into formal requirements and 'motivation' requirements.

Subjects which should *not* be included in the new recruit programme are:

- working hours
- overtime rules/pay rates
- pension and sickness schemes
- holiday entitlement
- social/sports club benefits
- discount purchase scheme
- and low interest/interest-free loans, etc.

All of these are part of the remuneration package and as such form part of the contract between employer and employee. These items should have been discussed and agreed *before* the recruit stepped through the door. If not, problems could arise.

A typical example involved a middle-ranking employee of a service industry company. This employee had been told before starting that he would be eligible for the company pension scheme. He was not told until after starting that he could not join the scheme until he had been in the company for nearly 12 months when the pension year started again. This was deeply resented by the employee who never forgot it and never ceased to distrust his employers. Perhaps he over-reacted but the fact was that he left after two years, still feeling resentful.

Assuming that all the contractual items have been properly dealt with, two checklists are required for the first day.

First day: Motivation checklist

- receptionist informed of newcomer (with name and department)
- future colleagues informed
- boss has allocated time for a welcome meeting
- boss or delegate ready to show newcomer round
- workplace ready (clean, tidy and fully equipped)
- arrangements made for lunch with colleagues
- explanation of informal group customs.

The person responsible for all the above should be the recruit's immediate boss.

First day: Formal requirements checklist

- clocking on/off system (if applicable)
- safety matters (e.g. use of protective clothing)
- security matters
- medical services/first aid
- and payroll matters (e.g. how to read the payslip).

These items can be dealt with either by the immediate boss or the personnel department.

There may, in addition, be other items for the personnel department (or company secretary) to attend to, such as signatures on pension forms and photographs for identification badges.

After the first day, during which the recruit has a lot to learn and remember, it is time to concentrate on the requirements of the job. Most recruits will more rapidly feel part of the company when they have work to do and a sense that they are contributing. There may be a need for some on-job training and general orientation which should be undertaken fairly gently perhaps during the second and third days. The recruit can then be taken through two more checklists.

First week: Motivation checklist

- confirmation that recruit is happy and has no work problems
- confirmation that recruit has no personal problems which concern the company
- invitation to take part in social events
- further explanation of purpose of job (if necessary)
- a talk about first impressions.
- is there anything the recruit needs or should be warned about?

Naturally, anything that is not satisfactory should be dealt with effectively and promptly. If, say, the recruit complains that his computer terminal is not working properly or he has not had adequate instructions on some part of the work the boss should do something about it straight away. It is not good enough to say, 'I'll look into the problem sometime', or, 'Yes it is pretty awful but I doubt if anything can be done about it.' This last statement comes from real life and confirmed a recruit's impression that her boss was just going through the motions and in reality could not care less about her problems.

Neglecting this checklist or anything arising from it is, in effect, saying to the recruit, 'Don't bother to tell me, you don't matter and I'm not interested.' If the checklist is fully and properly used, the recruit is given exactly the opposite impression and will be encouraged by it. This encouragement will be reflected in more and better work, which is good for the recruit, the company *and* the boss. In addition, the boss will avoid having a disgruntled subordinate who may well infect others with his misery.

Having dealt with these 'motivation' aspects, the boss can deal with the remaining formal matters.

First week: Formal requirement checklist

- fire drill and evacuation procedure
- opportunities for further education
- in-house training opportunities/schemes
- holiday rota
- suggestion scheme
- disciplinary procedure
- grievance procedure
- and savings scheme.

By the end of the first week, having dealt with all the relevant items on the checklists (and any items peculiar to the particular job or company which do not appear on the above lists), the employee should be feeling 'at home' and fully in the picture. The time is now right for the next and broader stage of induction. This is designed to ensure that the recruit is aware of the full company context in which he works. It is the presentation referred to under the type B company induction scheme and may include:

- company history and achievements
- description of the company's products/services
- who buys the products/services
- quality standards and reasons for them
- level of service which customers expect
- competitors and their products/services
- organisational structure of the company
- what the various departments do and why
- company policies (e.g. on promotion)
- company objectives and long-term plans.

In some companies this type of information can be adequately covered in a half-day session but others will allocate as much as two days to it.

The presentation will be most effective if various people speak about different things (e.g. the sales manager might talk about who the customers are, the managing director could discuss the quality standards and the personnel manager might outline the company history).

Slides or flip charts should be used to illustrate organisational structure and who's who. And samples of the product (or photographs) provided and explained. New recruits should also be given any company literature not already seen, and handout notes to act as an aide-memoire for future reference. Finally, time should be allowed for questions and discussion.

Some companies produce a video recording which is used instead of a personal presentation. This is not a particularly good idea as it is too impersonal and only allows for communication in one direction. It is also likely to be expensive to produce. However a good video can form a useful *part* of the presentation – or be used as a back-up to it. Induction presentations help in the settling-in process but are also a very necessary part of the training programme for most new employees. However the style should be relaxed and entertaining as well as informative.

Initial training

The presentation, having given the new recruit a framework in which to place his own work, should not be regarded as the end of the induction programme. Many new people, in some cases virtually all, will need some training in the skills and procedures required for their specific jobs.

Company standards
The purpose of this continued training is firstly to ensure that work is done to the standards required by the company and in the approved ways. If the employee is left to work out his own way of doing things – or to do his job in the way he did it in his previous company – it is likely that problems will arise. Clerical workers, for example, should be given instruction on how letters are to be written (style, layout and content). Your company may prefer an informal, modern style while the clerk may be used to the old '. . . your esteemed communication of the 14th ult . . .' way of doing things.

Some employees might also need to know how to complete forms and where to find the information to be entered. Not all forms are self-explanatory and instruction is often needed. An example is the form used by one company for recording running expenses for cars. This asked for 'Petrol consumption' and a box was provided for the answer. Some people entered a number of gallons while some entered miles per gallon. Failure to teach newcomers what is required can result in time and money being spent in correcting such errors, and frustration and annoyance all round.

Of course, it is not only in office work that training is needed. A skilled machine operator may need to know:

- how to requisition parts
- maintenance procedures
- job numbering systems
- and how to fill in job cards.

A warehouse worker may need to be shown:

- how the stock location system works
- the product or stock code system
- how to notify stock additions or decreases – and to whom
- and labelling systems.

Some people will need to be taught how to use the telephone. This is important because the response which customers and other callers receive when telephoning the company forms a major part of their impression. In the case of a potential customer calling for the first time, the response is *the* factor which governs the impression. A polite, 'John Smith, Sales Department, can I help you?' is far better than just 'Allo'.

Confidence

Continued training should also give the recruit a feeling of confidence. Any uncertainty as to how a job should be done has a demoralising effect on the employee. Not everyone is inclined to ask questions and young people in particular are reluctant to reveal their lack of knowledge. Even worse, when the employee has finally summoned up the courage to ask, he is then grumbled at or criticised for not knowing. This is by no means a rare reaction to a puzzled and anxious newcomer seeking help.

Productivity

Training will also make the new employee productive as soon as possible. During the settling-in period, output (i.e. correct and useful output) will be low, and this is part of the recruitment cost. If the length of this period can be reduced by some basic training the cost will be reduced.

Retaining new recruits

In addition, basic training will encourage the new recruit to stay with you. The first six months is a critical period in a new job. It is frequently the period during which the recruit decides whether or not to stay or look for another job.

The cost of *not* providing basic training

The following statements were made by junior members of a large department in an international company when asked to comment on their induction:

'Manuals or instructions were either absent or inadequate.'

'I cannot deal effectively with customers without training.'

'Confidence is lacked by many people and training is required to put it right.'

'I am not using the skills I learned elsewhere and it is a come-down to join this department.'

'My induction was bad and on the first day I was told by my colleagues that I would never get anywhere in the company and I felt like going home and never coming back.'

'My initial training was inadequate and I was not taught anything properly. The result was that I made mistakes.'

'There is a serious skills gap between the top people and the lower levels and when X is away there is no one to handle the work.'

'I am not entirely clear about what I am supposed to do.'

'The lack of training is unfair to the individuals and a lot of the time of the more experienced people is taken up in answering simple questions.'

'There are no manuals . . . we rely entirely on our memories.'

'I would like to learn more before I am thrown in at the deep end.'

'I feel that I am getting nowhere and I have had no proper training since being with the firm.'

'Three different people have shown me how to do the job and each of them has shown me a different way of doing it.'

'If I could have some proper training I would be more confident . . .'

These comments, some very forcibly put, in tones of resentment and anger, illustrate clearly the result of neglecting the training of new recruits and those who have been with the company for a few weeks or months. People subjected to this neglect often struggle through, learning expensively by trial and error. And some, perhaps most, will stay with the company as a result of inertia rather than enthusiasm for the job. In such cases all the effort put into finding good people is wasted by turning them into disaffected and mediocre people. The fault lies entirely with the company and its management – and the solution is quite simple.

However, before examining the solution it is worth considering one other real life example. In this case it was not a junior who commented on his induction. The person concerned was a well-paid, specialist graduate at middle management level. The following is part of a discussion which took place between the employee and a consultant who was looking for ways to improve the efficiency of the company concerned:

CONSULTANT: What are the main obstacles which prevent you from doing your job as effectively as you would wish?

EMPLOYEE: Undoubtedly the lack of training and explanation of policies. I had no induction training – not even how to find an envelope.

I have had no training since joining and it was a year before I discovered there was a manual which I could use. I got one from X when he left.

The lack of training meant that I was struggling and embarrassed to have to ask silly questions. My boss was too busy most of the time and I didn't like to bother him.

CONSULTANT: If you had had proper training in what way would this have been a benefit?

EMPLOYEE: Training would have had a great effect in saving lots of wasted time.

CONSULTANT: How much time?

EMPLOYEE: I don't know exactly. Perhaps as much as 50 per cent in the early days. The main thing is that I could have done the work more efficiently.

The conclusion in terms of the employee's feelings and the employer's profits are obvious.

A perceived lack of time to train is the most common reason for not doing it. It is not unusual for over-busy managers who *accept* the need to train their staff *and* realise that they will never cease being over-busy if they don't train them, to continue neglecting it. Time, they say, is not available.

On-job-training

Time *is* available if the right training system is used. This system, on-job-training (OJT), is based on small amounts of time which *can* be found. Before describing the OJT method it is important to state what OJT is not. It is not the method in which the new recruit is told, 'Sit next to Fred. He will show you what to do.' It is likely that Fred will have no time either, have no teaching skills, teach the wrong things, resent the burden placed on him, and/or treat the recruit as his personal slave to do all the rotten jobs. The result of Fred's ministrations is often a disaster.

The first steps in putting a real OJT scheme together is to determine *exactly* what it is that the trainee needs to learn. It is essential that general statements such as 'How to handle the office routines' or 'How to carry out product testing' are backed up by more precise and detailed definitions of tasks to be learned. For example, the office routines might include forecasting sales, by area, from customer records, and preparing a production plan for next month and calculating raw material costs.

Let us assume that these are the tasks that we want a trainee to learn. Having identified the tasks, the second step is to examine each one and break it down into its constituent parts. For instance, forecasting sales might break down as follows:

- take the sales records for each of the previous six months, drop the oldest of these and add the latest month's figures to the series.
- apply an exponential forecast formula to the figures to obtain a new forecast for three months ahead.
- add a weighting (positive or negative) to allow for higher sales in the summer months and lower sales in the winter months.
- distribute the forecast to sales managers, production managers and the transport department.

This breakdown will allow you to estimate the time required to teach each part of each subject:

- updating the figures   5 minutes
- applying the formula   20 minutes
- adding the weighting   15 minutes
- distributing the results   10 minutes

To teach all of these parts of the job in one go requires 50 minutes. Allowing for some wasted time it might take an hour – which the busy manager or supervisor may regard as impossible to find. However it will only take five minutes to teach the trainee how to update the figures. Five minutes is easy to find and is no more than the time taken up with occasional social chitchat. The longest period required (to teach him how to use the formula) is only 20 minutes – which is also achievable.

A programme can then be drawn up based on the estimated times.

Monday 9–9.05 a.m.	Updating
Tuesday 9–9.20 a.m.	Formula
Wednesday 9–9.15 a.m.	Weighting
Thursday 9–9.10 a.m.	Distribution

If the manager follows the programme – and sticks to it come what may – the trainee will have been taught the whole job by the end of the week. What is more, by 9.05 a.m. on Monday the trainee will be in a position to do the updating and will, as a result, be productive. If, for example, there are a number of products to be forecast there may be enough work to keep the trainee busy for the whole day. This has the advantage of providing a period for practice before moving on to the next part of the job.

It is important to ensure that the trainee has learned the job properly and some 10-minute review and revision sessions might be added to the programme. It is, in any case, highly desirable for the trainee to be supervised (*not* interfered with) and to be given the opportunity to ask for help and guidance if required. Not everyone can learn how to do something exactly right at the first attempt.

Another advantage is that the work to be done and the way it should be done is reviewed when the programme is being put together. This review will often reveal better ways to do the job and/or deviations from the agreed procedure which have crept in over the years. Sometimes work being done is found to be entirely unnecessary, such as the case where production reports were prepared for the production director and the chief accountant. The reports which each of these people received were identical, with the exception that the production director's version had an additional column showing 'percentage of production target' against each product. It was quickly realised that *both* recipients could receive the report showing the percentages. The chief accountant, who was not interested in the percentages, could ignore them. The result was one less report to be prepared and distributed.

Furthermore, by becoming productive at an early stage, the trainee will more rapidly feel 'at home' and part of the team. The converse – sitting around waiting to do something useful – is depressing and demotivating.

Ways to make OJT most effective

As in all forms of training there are good and less good ways of going about OJT. To obtain the best results it is necessary to avoid the things which inhibit learning and make use of techniques which encourage it. Here are some useful tips:

- prepare carefully. All the necessary forms, books, tools or whatever else is needed should be available and in good order.

- ensure that the session will not be interrupted. If the manager doing the teaching cannot be spared for 20 minutes or so then something is wrong with the organisation of the department.

- choose a suitable place for the session. Some OJT *must* be carried out at the workplace – which may be noisy, hot, dirty or otherwise none too pleasant. However, whenever possible a quiet comfortable place should be found. Discomfort is a distraction and any distraction inhibits learning.

- deal with each subject as a complete unit and teach them in a logical order. People who know a job inside out often muddle the sequence. If, for instance, a code number is needed you also need to explain where to find the number. This should be dealt with at the same time and not at the end with a comment such as 'By the way you'll find the code number in the code book on the shelf in Winnie's office.' The chances are that the trainee will not be sure which code number you are referring to – and in any case may not know what the book looks like, how to use it or where Winnie's office is.

- be careful with jargon. All companies have their own jargon – often in the form of initials. Terms like 'the flimsies', 'the 457s' and 'the NCAD list' (all taken from real life) need explanation. It is easy to use familiar jargon without realising that the trainee is baffled by it.

- be patient. Different people learn at different speeds. Going too fast is the greatest danger. The instructor must take the time required *and* avoid showing impatience. Signs of impatience, irritation or criticism will create fear in the mind of the trainee. And fear inhibits learning more than anything else.

- explain relevance and reason why. It is not always immediately apparent why something has to be done in a certain way – or at all. If the trainee doubts that something really matters he may skip over it and the teaching will not sink in.

- check progress regularly. It is important to ensure that the trainee has understood a subject *before* moving on to the next. Questions should be asked to check that he has not been left behind. The questions should be asked in a friendly manner with no hint of punishment for getting the answer wrong.

- be encouraging. A few words of encouragement can work wonders. Expressions such as 'Well done', 'Don't worry, everyone finds this difficult at first' and 'You are doing OK' will aid learning and help maintain the trainee's enthusiasm.

- use real-life examples and demonstrations. Examples of completed real-life work, pictures, diagrams and demonstrations are more effective than words alone. Explanation should be backed up with visual material to increase the speed of learning and the percentage which will be remembered.

- reinforce learning with supervised practice. Plenty of practice under gentle and friendly supervision will fix the subject in the trainee's mind.

- be enthusiastic. Enthusiasm is infectious. So too is any lack of it. Trainers, who know the subject inside out, may find themselves less than thrilled by the prospect of going over it again and again with successive trainees. Care must be taken to avoid showing any lack of interest on the trainer's part as this will become apparent to the trainee and can make the sessions dull and boring. Boredom is something else which inhibits learning.

This then is OJT – a first-class way to get new recruits started and to make them feel useful and wanted.

Induction and training dos and don'ts

- **do** remember what it feels like when starting a new job – especially if it is a first job. Check that you have done all you can to ensure that the newcomer is made to feel welcome and 'comfortable'.

- **do** have checklists – and use them – to ensure that each newcomer is properly informed and effectively introduced into the company.

- **do** have an induction scheme. **Don't** pay lip service to it as this can cost you a lot more time and money than the scheme itself.

- **don't** neglect initial training. Until the newcomer is taught the job (and the *right* way to do it) you are wasting money. **Do** use OJT.

7

THE RATE FOR THE JOB

THERE is an old saying that if you pay peanuts you get monkeys. The corollary of this must be that if you pay a fortune you will get geniuses. However it is most unlikely that either of these notions is wholly accurate. The question of the right pay for a job is much more complex and requires some careful attention from management.

It is certainly possible to buy someone's presence in your company. However this does not guarantee their enthusiasm or that they will produce good work. The quality of work and the employee's commitment must be earned by meeting a whole range of requirements other than pay. These requirements will be examined in Chapter 8.

The 'right' rate for a job depends on a number of factors, some of which are outside the control of the individual employer. Factors which employers cannot control include levels of personal taxation, cost of living indices, the market value of various skills, levels of unemployment, national wage and salary agreements, and the political strength of trade unions. In addition, in every country, there is a national environment within which the employer is operating and which will influence salary expectations. To make the whole thing more complicated, the environment will be constantly changing. The changes are often subtle and trends are not always easy to spot.

The environmental changes in the UK (not dissimilar to those in other industrialised countries) throughout the 1960s, '70s and '80s illustrate the problem. During the '60s and '70s rates of pay were largely controlled by 'the going rate' over which individual employers had little control. Government incomes policies, including 'freezes' on pay increases, were powerful influences, as was a fashion in some industries for paying a 'social wage'.

There has been a marked shift during the '80s to a position in which employers have much more influence and responsibility. The late '80s have seen the emergence of management freedom to adjust wage and salary rates to reflect the performance and contribution of individuals and the profitability of the business. There has also been a trend towards rewarding more senior people with profit-sharing and bonus schemes directly linked to company performances and additional to basic salary.

The salary policy

These environmental changes (which will continue), combined with the uncertainties about how individual employees will react to any given reward, mean that every company should have a salary policy. This is the only reliable way to maintain control in a changing world and to avoid ad hoc changes made at short notice, under pressure. The policy need not be complicated and, once agreed, should not be regarded as permanent. It will need to be reviewed from time to time to take account of changing circumstances, both internal and external. A rapidly growing company will need to review its policy more frequently than a relatively static one.

In fast-growing companies it is likely that, in addition to increasing numbers of employees, there will be new kinds of people coming into the business. For example, sales or computer specialists may be taken on and the former relationship between jobs and salaries will be disturbed. A policy is needed to ensure that expansion changes do not cause a clash between the longer-serving employees paid on a traditional basis and newcomers taken from a different market and demanding different treatment. In short the policy should be tailor-made to suit the needs of the business, its type and maturity.

A 'model' policy might be worded as follows:

Salary policy

Purpose
The purposes of the company wage/salary policy are:

- to recognise the value of each *job* relative to other jobs within the company and in comparison with similar jobs outside.
- to recognise the value of *individuals* and their contribution to the business.
- to determine wages and salaries according to the above.

Payment structure

Rates of pay will be based on job evaluation which will involve the participation of employees. The evaluations will be used to create job grades.

Each employee will be paid at least the minimum for his/her grade and position within the grade will reflect individual performance.

Starting salaries

Starting salaries will be determined by:

- the value to the business of the individual's relevant experience and skills.
- the value of the individual in the outside job market.
- value in comparison with existing employees in similar jobs.

Salary reviews

Salaries for all employees will be reviewed annually and increases, if any, will be paid with effect from 1 January.

Promotions

Any individual promoted from one grade to another will receive either the minimum salary for the new grade or a 10 per cent increase, whichever is the greater.

Movement within grades

Each employee will be made aware of salary ranges within each of the grades. Progress within a grade will be on a merit basis. A satisfactory performance will enable job-holders to reach the maximum for the grade in five years.

NB: Salary ranges within grades will be reviewed every two years.

Grievances

Any employee who feels that he/she has been treated unfairly either in the grading of his/her job or his/her position in the appropriate range has the right to appeal to his/her manager in the first instance. Should no agreement be reached, the employee has a right of appeal to the managing director whose decision will be final.

A policy along these lines, fully communicated to all employees, shows that the company has seriously considered how it intends to deal with salaries and is not relying on 'by guess or by God' methods. It ensures that both management and employees know where they stand. It also increases the chances of paying fair and sensible salaries and reduces the chances of losing good staff for money reasons. Having a policy can clearly save a great deal of heartache and trouble.

Job evaluation

There are various ways of going about job evaluation and there are a number of 'packaged' systems on offer from firms of consultants. It is not necessary to use these packages unless, for reasons of time, you prefer to employ the consultants to do the work for you. A relatively simple system can be used for which no special training is needed – and for which no fee need be paid. However a substantial measure of common sense will be required.

The system works as follows. Firstly, for each job to be graded, an up-to-date and agreed job description must be prepared. Note that it is the *job* which is being evaluated (and then graded) and not the individual doing the job.

Next, using the job description, a team of three or four people drawn from different parts of the company, will rate each part of the job against a list of attributes. The attributes might include:

- responsibility for staff
- responsibility for money
- degree of concentration required
- level of formal training needed
- minimum experience required
- potential damage caused by errors
- degree of contact with customers
- degree of contact with other outsiders
- and level of supervision necessary.

A points score of 0–5 is awarded for each attribute and the results may look something like this, taking a computer programmer and an accounts clerk as examples for illustration.

Attribute	Computer programmer	Accounts clerk
Responsibility for staff	0	1
Responsibility for money	0	3
Degree of concentration	5	3
Formal training needed	5	3
Experience needed	2	2
Potential damage from errors	5	2
Contact with customers	0	0
Contact with others	1	1
Level of supervision needed	3	4
TOTAL:	21	TOTAL: 19

The scores given will, of course, depend upon the requirements of each job in relation to each of the attributes. In the example, the accounts clerk's job scores 1 for responsibility for staff while the computer programmer scores 0. This is because the accounts clerk's job might require the incumbent to train a junior from time to time. Programmers work alone and, in the case of this (mythical) company, are not required to be responsible for anyone else's work. By contrast, the job of a programmer requires a higher level of concentration (5) than the job of accounts clerk (3).

The resulting totals are not far apart, indicating that overall the two jobs are fairly close in value. This suggests that in the grading which follows evaluation they might both be in the same grade or in adjacent ones with a degree of overlap. This overlap is illustrated in Figure 7.1, which shows how a grading scheme might work in terms of salary ranges.

Overlap is important in that it provides a means to reward long service, and the experience which goes with it, in the case of an employee who is not suitable for promotion to a higher-graded job. Thus, for example, the accounts clerk's job may be given grade C. A wholly satisfactory employee may do the job for many years but still not be suitable for promotion to grade D – the grade for senior accounts clerk. However the experience represented by

Salaries and grades

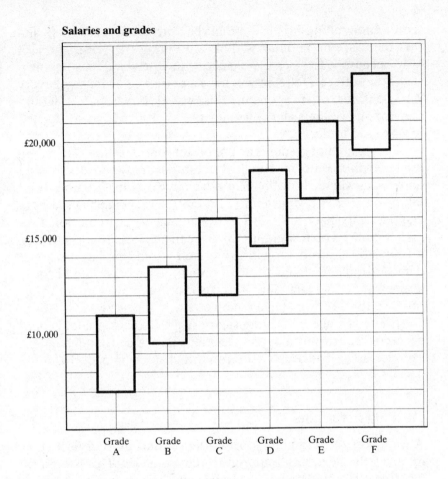

the years of service can be rewarded by moving the clerk up to the top of grade C. This can mean that for a time the clerk is actually paid more than a senior clerk with less experience. In turn the senior clerk has a higher ceiling for his grade, which, with the passage of time, means he will first approach and then overtake his junior (though more experienced) colleague.

Double-checking the grades for fairness

When all jobs have been given scores the totals are compared and each job allocated a grade. In some companies, in order to show that justice has been done, a team of two umpires will scrutinise the scores and gradings to ensure that the outcome is reasonable and that there are no anomalies. This precaution is a sensible one if only because it reduces the chance of any personal bias having a significant effect. No team will have a perfect knowledge of every job and if, for instance, one member was at some time a programmer (or an accounts clerk) he may press for higher scores for the job he used to do.

The number of grades is an important consideration. Too many grades will result in small differentials between them and employees will see little financial advantage in being promoted and taking on greater responsibility. In addition very small increases in responsibility may have to be accompanied by promotion to a higher grade. Too few grades can have the reverse effect – making it seem too difficult to gain promotion – and this has a distinct demotivating effect. As a rule of thumb, five grades should cover all jobs up to and including supervisor or foreman, with a further three or four for the management strata.

The final stage, allocating salary ranges to each grade, should be carried out by senior management as a wholly independent exercise. (This is discussed later in this chapter on page 102.)

Flexibility of grades

A common objection to job evaluation and grading is that it removes the flexibility required to reward merit. This is entirely incorrect. The grading has resulted from a valuation of each *job* on the basis of what it entails. The individual worker is not *directly* affected by it.

The impact on the individual results from the salary range awarded to the grade and the position of the worker within that range.

There should be ample flexibility to move an individual more (or less) rapidly up the range for his grade in response to the effort and contribution he has made. Employee X for example, having worked significantly better than colleague Y, may be given an increase of 15 per cent at the annual review. Colleague Y may only receive 5 per cent.

Another way to build flexibility into the salary system is to apply fast stream and slow stream limits to a standard salary range. This is illustrated in the table overleaf. It will be seen that an

Fast and slow streams within grade B

Grade B – Salary range

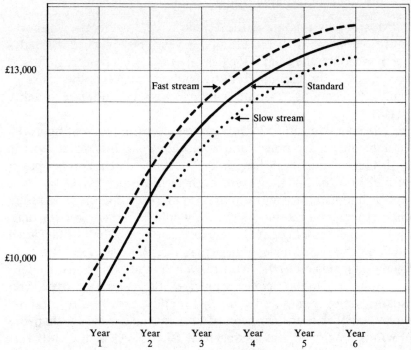

employee in the fast stream will, in year 2, be paid more than fellow employees on the standard range and on the slow stream. Using this method allows an exceptional worker to be placed in a position in which, even if he receives the same *percentage* increase as his colleagues, he will always be better off in cash terms. The streaming system can easily be varied to suit differing circumstances or requirements by changing the gap between the standard salary range and the slow or fast stream.

Fairness

In his book *The Management of Remuneration* (Institute of Personnel Management, 1983) Ian Smith said, 'It is not total pay which excites people but pay comparisons.' He went on to say:

> The willingness of people to stay in the organisation and, more importantly perhaps, their level of contribution to com-

pany performances, are more dependent on 'relative' levels of remuneration than absolute levels . . .

Most of us recognise the scenario where George, hitherto entirely content with his £12,000 a year, discovers that Gladys (who is doing the same job) is on £14,000. George suddenly becomes wholly discontented. This phenomenon is the cause of many resignations, disputes, human misery and poor-quality work.

The problem can be largely prevented by implementing a well thought-out salary policy and *communicating* the results to the staff. George might not have been upset by Gladys's higher pay if he had known that they were both on the same grade but that Gladys had had three more years' experience. If George had fully understood the grading system he would also have known that, everything else being equal, he could also reach the £14,000 level when he had the same level of experience. If he works better than Gladys and gets on to the fast stream he might even overtake her.

Another familiar scenario involves the good employee who asks for more money, does not get it and leaves as a result. The replacement is then taken on at an even higher salary than the previous employee was asking for. To the rest of the staff this merely confirms the stupidity of the management ('and it serves them right to have to pay even more').

The problem can be largely avoided by keeping up with the job market and making sure that salary ranges are up to date and realistic. Sometimes the opportunity is taken after a resignation to employ someone with more experience or skills than the leaver. This can justify a higher salary, which should be clearly explained to the staff. Knowing why a decision has been made can often make 'unfair' situations seem fair.

Setting the salary range for each grade

As already stated, the task of deciding on the salary limits within each grade is not something to be carried out by the job evaluation team (although in many smaller companies, one owner-manager will have to deal with all these matters.) Management (whether a single person or a team) must decide the pay scale structure since they are responsible for formulating policy and ensuring that the policy is implemented. In addition, whatever the gradings may be for the various jobs, the salary scales have a direct impact on company cash flow and, ultimately, on profits. These are matters for management decision.

Managers are also responsible for ensuring that good staff do not leave the company as a result of salary scales being unreasonably low. Conversely, budget and profitability demands impose the need to avoid paying unnecessarily high salaries. What then are the factors which must be taken into account when setting the scales for the grades? The main factors are listed below.

Supply and demand

The company salary scales must be adequate to attract and keep the people the business needs. This is in the context of a competitive market in which rates of pay are to a great extent determined by supply and demand. Computer staff, for instance, have been in short supply for many years, with the result that market rates have been subject to sudden and sometimes dramatic rises. Companies which have not responded to these rises have seen mass resignations – sometimes with serious consequences.

A fairly dramatic example was provided by British Airways in 1988. Certain computer staff, skilled in the airline 'transaction processing facility' (tpf) were being offered pay rises ranging from £5,000 to a doubling of salary by rival airlines. Turnover for tpf staff rose from 10 per cent to 17 per cent in three months. To counter these losses, British Airways came up with a special deal which offered an extra year's pay as a bonus for staying with the company for three years.

The 'big bang' in the City of London in 1987 saw similar effects. Market makers, money dealers and the like found themselves in great demand as American and other foreign companies opened for business in London. For many companies, staff movements were frequent and costly. Press reports of five- and even six-figure 'golden hellos' were an indication of the pressures on employers at the time. The 'crunch' for the employees came after the October Crash in 1987 when trading volumes fell and redundancies became commonplace. The golden hello was replaced by the swift, sudden and low-priced farewell.

In both these examples the staff involved have tended to be relatively young. And this raises another dimension which managers must think about. Young people (say those under 30) tend to be more mobile than their older colleagues – though this is not a good reason for failure to keep up with market rates for the older people!

Managers need to be aware of the local employment situation and market rates in the area. Local and national surveys (or simply keeping an eye on the job advertisements) will be a useful guide, as will advice from recruitment agencies and consultants. It can also be helpful to compare notes with other employers in the area – if possible on a regular basis.

Perception and expectation

Whether or not the employee is satisfied with his salary will largely depend on his perception of his job, combined with his expectations of the rate at which his salary should increase with experience. Keeping the individual in the company may depend on the speed at which his salary increases each year and, as far as possible, managers must keep themselves aware of expectations. This does not mean awarding absurdly high increases to satisfy absurdly high expectations but nor does it mean ignoring individual feelings. Remember, it is the employee who decides whether or not to look for a job offering more money.

Motivation

Whether or not money motivates people to work harder and/or better is an old subject for debate. The argument seems to boil down to two major factors. Firstly, an increase in reward has only a short-term effect on the enthusiasm of the employee. Secondly, reward below the level which the employee perceives as being just and fair will positively *demotivate*.

In other words, pay too little and the employee loses enthusiasm. Pay too much and you may gain some *temporary* lift in effort. At first glance this looks like bad news for managers but, on reflection, it confirms that it is unnecessary to pay absurdly high salaries and little may be gained from it in terms of work quantity and quality.

Employees who work on a commission or piecework basis are also affected by non-money factors. There is ample evidence to show that payment by result does not always ensure good-quality work and long service. Sales people, for example, have been known to 'cut corners', mislead customers and misrepresent the product or service to make a sale and gain the commission.

Union agreements

Company or national agreements with trade unions relieve individual managers of making decisions on pay rates. Contrary to popular belief, many of the larger companies therefore welcome the involvement of powerful unions who 'keep the staff in line'.

For many years a major British company had a staff association which bargained with management on pay and conditions. The staff association was not averse to the company awarding merit increases to individuals. Then a small group of militant employees began to agitate for union membership and the staff association was dissolved in favour of membership of an active and aggressive trade union.

All went well until some members of staff proposed that certain jobs in the company merited greater reward. Management referred them to the union who promptly sent a representative to sort things out. The representative gave the employees concerned a dressing-down and made it clear that only the union could approach the management. The spokesman for the employees was told that rates of pay were 'none of your bloody business'. Sadly, the management were quite happy with this state of affairs.

The proprietor of a small engineering company (about 25 employees) also welcomed union membership for much the same reason. 'Once the rates are agreed that's it,' he said. 'I might pay a penny or two an hour over the official rate but I don't have to worry about each individual employee badgering me for special deals.'

Using charts

Having taken into account all the factors which are relevant, the manager or managers deciding on the salary ranges will find it useful to illustrate them on charts or graphs. Such a visual representation makes it easier to communicate the results to all concerned and will also indicate any anomalies. The diagram on the next page illustrates a typical situation, including employees who are paid 'too much' or 'too little'.

As the chart shows, there are a number of employees whose present salary is outside the range for their grade. This could either mean that the ranges are out of step with reality or that a number of employees are being incorrectly rewarded for the job they do. To solve the problem, the ranges for some or all of the grades could be changed to take in some of the anomalies. Alternatively, the

Actual salaries by grade, showing the 'degree of fit'

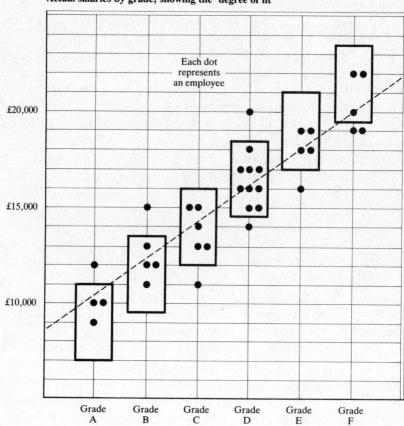

ranges might be regarded as fair or reasonable. In the latter case the employees whose salary falls outside the range for their grade will need some special attention.

If you decide to adjust the ranges a useful way to approach it is to draw a line through the middle of the scatter (the dotted line on the chart) so that roughly half the dots fall above the line and half below. (NB: In real life the line will almost certainly be curved to allow for a greater number of employees at the lower levels of salary.) The salary ranges can now be re-calculated by fixing the upper and lower levels at between 20 and 25 per cent above and below the line respectively (as illustrated in Figure 7.2.) Such a re-calculation may result in all the employees fitting into the range for their respective grades but it is likely that there will still be at least one or two anomalies.

Sorting out the anomalies

Employees who are paid above the range for their grade present the most difficult problem. They may have to be clearly told that they are in this position and that future salary awards will be strictly limited (or zero) until such time as they are promoted to a higher grade or the range for their grade is increased.

Quite frequently, however, such apparently overpaid people are actually found to be quite properly paid for what they do. It could be the case, for instance, that an individual carries out some work which belongs to a higher grade. Consideration can be given to promoting him to the higher grade or treating him as a special case until jobs are re-evaluated.

Those employees who are paid below the range for their grade should be promptly brought up to at least the minimum figure. It is not uncommon for managers to duck this issue by saying that the gap is too great and can only be put right over a number of years. Quite apart from any questions of ethics (or conflict with the agreed salary policy), this will cause resentment among the unfortunate employees concerned and concern among the others. Staff loyalty and trust always suffer when this line of action is taken and it is never worth it in the long term.

Monitoring progress

It is a fundamental mistake to confuse staff appraisals with salary structure considerations and salary awards. The appraisal system – based on six-monthly or annual interviews between manager and subordinate – has the objective of identifying the employee's strengths and weaknesses and agreeing on a programme to improve future performance. This process should be a frank and objective one aimed at reaching constructive agreements to the benefit of the company and the employee.

Recognising the weaker areas which both parties will try to improve is an essential part of the appraisal process. And if the results of the appraisal interview include a recommendation on salary increases then the employee can be forgiven for not being willing to admit his weaknesses. This is why appraisal schemes which are linked to salary frequently fail. (More information on appraisal schemes is given on page 151.)

Consideration of an employee's progress up the salary range

for his grade should be dealt with entirely separately – possibly involving a confidential report prepared by his manager. Such a report should be based on a uniformly applied system. The simplest approach is to use a form listing various qualities (see opposite).

This method is much superior to the 'freestyle' report in that the form acts as a checklist to remind the manager of the various qualities which should be taken into consideration. Without such a checklist the report can easily be distorted by one or two factors. It is natural, for example, for a manager to be irritated by repeated lack of punctuality on the part of an employee who is otherwise performing well. This irritation could cause the manager to overlook the employee's good side and give a general impression which is less than fair.

Although this system has an attractive simplicity, a more sophisticated approach has been gaining favour during the 1980s. This involves concentrating less on a range of personal qualities and more on the achievement of specific objectives. Each employee's job description contains objectives, and their performance is measured against them. However not all targets can be specified in quantitative terms which makes it difficult to measure performance. Some qualitative assessment may also be required, involving an element of subjective judgement. For example, an employee may be required to work 'in co-operation' with someone in another department. Whether or not this is achieved satisfactorily may be hard to determine. One way to do it is to write out the attributes of another employee who is regarded as satisfactory in this respect and compare them with those of the employee being assessed.

One system, recommended by a well-known firm of management consultants, is fairly widely used. This includes such measures of performance as expressing subjective judgements on a rating scale of 1–10, results against time limits (e.g. for completion of a project or regular tasks) and ratios of errors per employee per day.

Several employers combine performance assessment with the more traditional merit rating systems, and at least one major international bank decides bonus payments by the former and general salary increases by the latter.

Fast-stream salaries

A study carried out in the UK by the PA Consulting Group, reported in 1989, looked into trends in graduate employment.

EMPLOYEE PERFORMANCE REPORT

NAME _____   JOB TITLE _____   DEPT _____

	Excellent	Good	Fair	Poor	Not applicable
Punctuality					
Accuracy					
Leadership					
Planning and organisation					
Co-operation					
Dependability					
Initiative					
Communication skills					

OVERALL ASSESSMENT   Above average ☐   Average ☐   Below average ☐

COMMENTS _____

_____

_____

Signed _____   Date _____

109

Among other things the study investigated the differences in salaries paid to 'adequate' or 'average' employees and those judged to be 'high flyers'. The study findings showed the following levels of premium* paid to the high flyers after five years:

Industry	Percentage
Banking and building societies	36.7
Oil and gas	25.5
Food, drink and tobacco	22.8
Computers, electronics	19.1
Insurance	18.8
Engineering	15.5
Distribution and retail	14.3
Professional services	7.4

The average rate was 18 per cent.

The very low premium paid to high flyers in the professional services (7.4 per cent) may indicate that lawyers, accountants and the like seek some other inducement to stay with their firms. This could well be the prospect of a partnership which, in the long run, could be financially very attractive and also offer considerable status satisfaction. At the other end of the scale, banks and building societies seem to pay highly to keep their high performers. This too may be associated with status prospects – which are lower in an industry notorious for reserving its board room places for people who are members of an 'in-group'.

These figures show a wide range of employers trying to decide how much their fast-stream employees should be paid, over and above their less successful colleagues. It could be dangerous or unnecessary to place too much weight on the average figure of 18 per cent. The figures indicate that the nature of the business and the industry group are very important factors.

Another factor which should be considered (the high-flying employees will certainly consider it) is the chance of making it to board level in a small firm. Family firms, in particular, need to think seriously about this if they have a policy (spoken or otherwise) of reserving top jobs for family members. If the high flyers

---

* A premium could be a percentage, or a fixed sum, or a variation on these.

believe this to be the case a substantial premium may be necessary to keep them. And their enthusiasm may not be retained by money alone if other 'satisfiers' such as status, recognition and 'job satisfaction' are denied them.

Perks and benefits

Any employee benefits offered by the company should be taken into account when working out a salary structure. It should not be supposed, however, that the cost to the company is necessarily equal to the value placed on the benefits by the employees. For example, a major retail company allows its staff to make purchases at a substantial discount. The company sells a wide range of products, some of which are used regularly in most households. It would be reasonable to suppose therefore that the discount scheme would be highly valued by the employees.

According to an informal survey of 12 employees at one branch of the company, it seems that little value is in fact placed on the scheme. The people questioned were mature women, all of whom did most of the shopping for their households. Only one of them definitely valued the scheme and had realised that the discount represented a form of income. Some of the others did not even trouble to make use of the discount opportunity – one saying that she 'couldn't be bothered'.

It appeared that none of the employees had been attracted to the job by the scheme and it did not seem to be a significant factor in retaining them. The manager of the branch confirmed this impression and said that although he always mentioned the discount scheme to job applicants it appeared to have little effect.

Other benefits can also be regarded very differently by the company and the employee. Pension and health insurance schemes, for instance, are given scant attention by young people who are much more concerned with the amount shown on the payslip. Company cars are regarded as nothing exceptional in a number of jobs and, however costly they may be to the company, the employee looks more closely at the salary offered. Perversely, the same employees, having come to expect a car, would not consider a job which did not provide one.

So you need to consider how much employees will be influenced by benefits when working out the salary ranges. The value of a benefit in real terms should also be made clear to employees. For example, it could be pointed out that if an employee spends £20 per week in a company store and receives a 20 per cent discount, this is worth about £200 per annum (after tax in many cases). A company car can be valued in thousands of pounds.

The view that employees take will largely depend on how old they are and the social group to which they belong. Cheap mortgages are highly valued by bank employees in the house-buying age range who, by the very nature of their employment, are well able to work out and appreciate their value. Health insurance is more highly valued by older employees who, with the passing years, have begun to view lengthy illness as more of a real possibility. They will therefore place a high value on payment during sickness and private hospital treatment.

Whatever the views of the employees may be, there is concrete evidence that more and more British companies are offering a wider range of fringe benefits than in the past. Anecdotal evidence suggests the same trend in Germany and France.

A study carried out in Britain by the Alfred Marks group and the magazine *Personnel Today* showed that about 50 per cent of employers estimate that fringe benefits make up more than 20 per cent of payroll costs. The study, which covered 450 companies and was published in November 1988, indicated which benefits were most frequently provided for office staff. The list included:

Benefit	Percentage of employers
Sick and maternity pay	100
Pension scheme	96
Help with further education	94
Life or accident insurance	86
Long-service awards	79
Canteen or dining room	68
Medical insurance	64
Discount buying	48
Bonus system	38
Share option/profit sharing	37
Sports club	33

There were, in addition, a number of less frequently occurring benefits, including hairdressing allowance, payments on marriage, office outings and nursery facilities. Meal vouchers were offered by only 11 per cent of employers – possibly because of the tax which recipients are obliged to pay if this benefit exceeds an amount decreed by the Government.

Unfortunately no study appears to have been carried out to find out what the employees think of the perks on offer, or the effect on recruitment and retention of staff before and after any particular goodies are introduced. The nearest thing to evidence that perks are valued by employees (or at least some perks by some employees) was a study carried out in 1988 by Henley Management College. Commenting on the study, *Personnel Management* (November 1988) said that opportunities for further education, job training, development and *recognition* were key motivators. It was also noted that employees 'clearly distinguished' these benefits from the more traditional ones such as transport, welfare and recreational facilities. The study claimed that most employers could increase satisfaction by more generous provision of perks.

Bonuses and profit sharing

Various forms of payment, related to profits and in addition to basic salary, have become increasingly popular throughout the '70s and '80s. These schemes are normally on a group basis and are fundamentally different from the older 'payment by results' systems used for many years with shop floor workers. The shop floor schemes are directly related to the individual worker and his personal level of productivity. Group schemes, however, are related to the performance of the business as a whole and do not reflect the productivity of any individual employee.

It is doubtful whether there is any clear merit in such schemes. Payments are rarely close enough in time to the achieved group performance to make much impression on the individual (whose own efforts are in any case submerged in the efforts of the whole group). The individual is unlikely to relate his own performance to the bonus he receives and any incentive effect is thus negated.

In some cases the annual profit-sharing bonus has come to be regarded by staff as merely a deferred payment of salary. Many would prefer a higher salary and no bonus at all.

It seems pointless to risk spoiling a sound salary scheme by complicating it with bonuses and the attendant potential for quarrels over percentage shares of the amount allocated. The system has at times been used simply to discourage employees from leaving. The theory is that people will stay on to receive their bonus. This they do – and leave immediately afterwards. In the end, unless a bonus scheme improves output in terms of quality and quantity and is entirely self-financing, it achieves nothing which a good basic salary will not achieve.

The same comments apply to the provision of shares in the company. Many, if not most, of such shares are sold as soon as possible by the recipients, who are not interested in share ownership.

It is perhaps only at executive levels that receiving shares in the company is of any interest, but even then the shares are not regarded in any special or motivating way. They are probably viewed in the same way as any other share, except that in some countries there is a tax advantage in being 'paid' in employer's shares rather than cash.

There is, though, another aspect of the incentive addition to salary which was pointed out by Terry Lunn, Personnel Director of Joshua Tetley & Son, in an article in *The Sunday Times* (28 October 1988). Referring to promotional gifts, holiday trips and the like, Lunn stated:

> It's not only the award's value that acts as a motivation but also the pleasure of being recognised as the best waitress of the month or as the team that achieved highest productivity. We tend to do well what others applaud us for doing.

In other words, the really encouraging thing about a reward is the recognition of achievement that it represents. This can apply as much to an increase in salary as it can to a bonus, a free holiday or a batch of shares.

Dos and don'ts of salaries and benefits

- **do** have a company policy for wages and salaries – however simple.
- **do** translate the policy into effective and practical application through the use of job evaluation, grading and salary ranges.

- having agreed the policy and put it into operation, **don't** sit back and do nothing more. Regular review and update is essential.

- **do** relate your salary grades to external as well as internal factors and don't neglect the employees' perception of what is fair and just.

- **don't** assume that money alone will guarantee good work or commitment.

- **do** use charts and graphs to clarify your salary structure – and to communicate it to everyone in the company.

- **don't** use staff appraisals for salary review purposes. **Do** create a separate system for salary awards.

- **don't** assume that employees will value benefits as much as you do. Young people in particular are more likely to be interested in what is on the payslip.

- **do** be careful with profit-sharing bonuses and similar incentives. There is little convincing evidence that they improve either quantity or quality of output.

$$8$$

KEEPING THEM – AND KEEPING THEM ENTHUSIASTIC

THE previous chapter dealt with the financial rewards for doing a job. It was suggested that paying more money was not always a reliable way of retaining people *and* maintaining their commitment to the job. In *The Management of Remuneration* Ian Smith proposes an alternative to money alone:

> Remuneration is a reward which needs to be accompanied by other types of reward, particularly if remuneration is to be effectively displayed as a means of retaining and motivating people . . . Wages, salaries, company cars, pensions and the like should be 'mixed in' with status, job satisfaction and other behavioural elements in a synergistic effect which brings forward the required levels of effort and/or contributions from employees.

Assessing the problem

This chapter is concerned with those 'behavioural elements' which will be paramount in deciding whether or not you can keep your good people. The first step is to see whether you have a problem and, if so, how big it is.

Measuring the turnover rate

To what extent a company has a retention problem can be determined by listing the causes of resignation and then calculating turnover for the 'controllable' reasons. Resignations fall into two categories, as shown on the next page.

Controllable reasons:

- remuneration
- nature of work
- promotion/prospects
- physical conditions
- relationships with colleagues
- working hours
- and job satisfaction.

Uncontrollable reasons:

- domestic problems
- marriage/pregnancy
- illness/disability
- travelling difficulties
- and housing problems.

The resignations for controllable reasons are the ones to concentrate on since, to a greater or lesser extent, the company could have done something to prevent them – and can prevent them in the future. Taking, say, a year's records, the number of resignations are entered into the following equation:

$$\frac{\text{No. of resignations}}{\text{Average number employed during the year}} \times 100 = \text{Annual employee wastage}$$

Thus, if 30 resignations occurred in a year when the average number on the payroll was 145, the employee wastage was:

$$\frac{30}{145} \times 100 = 20.7\%$$

Ideally, the figure would be 0 per cent, implying that the company is not only recruiting effectively but is also keeping its recruits. In real life a zero loss would be a remarkable performance but what is an 'acceptable figure'? There is no 'right' answer to this and one personnel director gave the response 'it all depends'.

This reply is not as unhelpful as it may at first appear. The experience of personnel specialists – backed up by the results of a number of surveys – shows that the acceptable (or, at least, expected figure) varies according to employee age, location and the degree of specialisation in the job.

Experience shows that among young people in junior grades a turnover rate of up to 20 per cent is to be expected in cities and larger towns. The figure may be about 10 to 12 per cent in smaller towns and rural areas. Specialists such as accountants, computer analysts and information technology experts can also be expected to change jobs fairly frequently, often to gain experience and in response to market forces in the form of higher pay elsewhere.

According to a survey of accountancy firms in the UK (commissioned by Robert Walters Associates and published early in 1989), over 60 per cent of younger staff seek jobs in industry or the City. In other words, having been trained in accounting, they move on to non-accountancy employers. The most frequently stated reason for these moves is to obtain higher salaries. Turnover rates for non-specialists and older people in clerical grades can be expected to be much lower.

Deciding on an acceptable turnover figure therefore means considering the type of people employed and where your business is located. In any event it is worth having a benchmark figure as a means of measuring your own performance. It can also tell you whether improvement can realistically be expected, however desirable it may be.

A wastage figure taken in successive years or at six-monthly intervals is often a valuable indication as to whether or not management is doing its job properly. A steadily maintained low figure or a decline year by year suggests that things are going well. A rising trend indicates an urgent need to do some self-evaluation in the board room and to have a cold hard look at how employees are being treated.

Clearly, the wastage figures can provide more precise information if you calculate them for different groups of employees. This allows for the expected differences between age groups or between senior and junior employees, among others.

You may also wish to compare the results between departments and between male and female employees. A higher figure for female employees could indicate that they are being denied opportunities which their male colleagues receive. And variations between departments which are basically similar in employee type can point to a need for improvement in management style.

Useful comparisons can also be made between shop floor and office staff and between skilled and non-skilled people in the same departments. These more specific comparisons are often helpful in pinpointing areas of poor management, particularly failure to apply company policies uniformly over the whole workforce.

Another interesting figure is the number of dismissals as a percentage of the workforce. Every employee dismissed for reasons of discipline or unsuitability is an implication that recruitment was less than satisfactory and/or that leadership is not up to the mark.

In looking at these figures, management must take great care not to lull themselves into complacency by giving easy excuses. One manager, when asked to comment on some people who had resigned, said, 'They were all lazy. They did us a favour by leaving.' This is a dangerous attitude as there is ample evidence that very few people are lazy. As has been said before, there are quite a lot who are unmotivated or demotivated and therefore *appear* to be lazy.

In *The Human Side of Enterprise*, Douglas McGregor argued that: 'The expenditure of physical and mental effort in work is as natural as rest and play.' He also stated that: 'The average man learns, under proper conditions, not only to accept but to seek responsibility.' These are two of the six statements he makes in his theory Y assumption – part of his famous X and Y theory of management. (This theory is described more fully on page 166.)

Measuring the 'stability rate'

Measuring staff turnover can be turned on its head by working out how long people stay rather than what percentage leave. The result is known as the 'stability rate' and is calculated by using the formula:

$$\frac{\text{No. of employees with 12 months service or over}}{\text{Total number employed a year ago}} \times 100$$

Some employers find this a more helpful, or more optimistic, way to examine the situation. The calculation can be varied by working out the stability rate over different lengths of time – five years is a popular choice.

Once again the question crops up: 'What should the stability rate be?' And once again the answer depends on a number of factors including, to some extent, the industry you are in. The survey by the PA Consulting Group (mentioned in Chapter 7) also looked at the percentages of recruits who were still employed by the same company five years after being taken on. PA found significant differences between industries.

Industry	Percentage	Premium
Banks and building societies	46	(36.7)
Oil and gas	72	(25.5)
Food, drink and tobacco	44	(22.8)
Computers, electronics	57	(19.1)
Insurance	61	(18.8)
Engineering	44	(15.5)
Distribution and retail	49	(14.3)
Professional services	(not available)	

The figures in brackets are those given in Chapter 7 for the percentage premium paid to high flyers. Comparison of the two sets of figures shows that there is little correlation between the premium paid to the whizz-kids and the industry stability rate. Overall, the stability rate for all the industries surveyed was 52 per cent.

Why do people leave?

Managers must *always* look at the causes of resignation from the employee's viewpoint. Even if the boss completely disagrees with the employee's opinion, it is the employee's perception which counts. No amount of justification can alter the facts if good people are leaving – and continue to leave.

In Chapter 5 the comments of a group of employees on their induction were quoted. The same group gave their views on other aspects of management in their department. This is what they said:

'There is a lack of appreciation for a job well done.'

'The senior people are not always approachable and the juniors find it difficult to talk to them about their problems.'

'Our abilities are not appreciated . . .'

'There are unnecessary rules . . .'

'In the past juniors have been regarded as cannon fodder and no one cared if they left.'

'There is a lack of communication and we often find out that a change has been arranged when we hear it from someone in another department.'

'There is a lack of discipline . . . I am uncomfortable in the present environment.'

'The secretaries are treated as battery hens.'

'The reason for the high staff turnover is that there are no prospects of promotion and it seems stupid that we are recruiting A level people for jobs which do not require that level of intelligence.'

'We need a consistent and agreed departmental policy on both behaviour and standards of performance.'

'I want an opportunity to prove myself.'

'I want an opportunity to improve myself.'

'The work is boring . . .'

'I don't get the responsibility I would like.'

'There is no delegation and the good work, I mean the interesting work, is kept by those above.'

'It would be nice to know that we are appreciated.'

These comments, all from one group of people, reveal just about every basic error which managers can make. Getting it right – and keeping the people happy, productive and appreciated is what the rest of this chapter is all about.

Solving the problem

Management style

In 1967 Dr Rensis Likert of the University of Michigan published *The Human Organisation – Its Management and Value*. This remarkable book, the result of a massive amount of research, identified four styles of management. Likert believed that only one of these styles was ideal for the company which is concerned about profits *and* people – the demands of both being entirely compatible. Likert's four styles are listed below.

1. The exploitative – authoritative
Decisions are imposed on subordinates, motivation is characterised by threats, high levels of management have great responsibility but lower levels have virtually none. There is very little communication and no teamwork.

2. The benevolent – authoritative
Leadership is by a condescending form of master-servant trust, motivation is mainly by reward, managers feel responsible but lower levels do not. There is little communication or teamwork.

3. The consultative
Leadership is by superiors who have substantial (but not complete) trust in their subordinates, motivation is by reward and some involvement. A high proportion of personnel feel responsible for achieving organisational goals, there is some communication and a moderate amount of teamwork.

4. The participative – group
Leadership is by superiors who have complete trust in their subordinates, motivation is by economic rewards based on goals which have been set in participation. Personnel at all levels feel responsible for organisational goals, there is much communication and co-operative teamwork.

At first glance, Likert's fourth style seems Utopian and unattainable, given that managers are only human. But the participative group style *is* attainable – and some managers have succeeded in achieving it. Some of the key actions required to achieve the fourth style are:

- to ensure that staff have no fears or inhibitions in discussing work with the manager. In particular staff should be encouraged to talk about problems *and* errors with the boss, who does not show anger but instead discusses the problem in a helpful, friendly and constructive way.

- frequently involving the staff in finding solutions to problems. The ideas of staff should be encouraged, not only because no manager has a monopoly of genius but also because the staff are more likely to support the solution if they are involved in choosing it.

- motivating by giving rewards and recognition as a result of achievement of *agreed* objectives – and avoiding threats and punishment.

- constantly communicating decisions and the reasons for them to all staff and encouraging the flow of communication upwards and horizontally.

- openly discussing information received and encouraging staff to discuss openly any situations and circumstances which affect them.

- ensuring that subordinates' problems are known and understood.

- encouraging co-operation and teamwork.

- encouraging the view that problems should be shared and material support given in order to keep things going.

- involving the staff in decision-making to the lowest hierarchical level possible.

- setting goals by group discussion.

- delegating control and monitoring of performance to all levels – as far as possible allowing individuals to monitor their own performance against agreed standards.

- using performance results as a means for self-guidance – never using them to police or punish.

These actions on the part of a manager will go a long way towards achieving the commitment of employees. However researchers other than Likert have identified further requirements.

Job content and context

In 1959 F. Herzberg carried out work among accountants and engineers to find out which factors created satisfaction and which caused dissatisfaction. The factors shown to be crucial in creating satisfaction – and which had the power to motivate positively – were all concerned with the *content* of the job. They included:

- sense of achievement
- recognition
- amount of responsibility
- prospects of advancement
- and interesting work.

It is interesting to compare these results with the comments of the dissatisfied staff quoted earlier in this chapter. Some 29 years had elapsed since Herzberg's findings were published but the comments show that human nature has not changed at all.

Herzberg also identified factors concerned with the *context* of the job. These will cause dissatisfaction if they are not properly handled. However, even if dealt with to perfection, these factors will not motivate. They include:

- company policy and administration
- supervision
- interpersonal relationships
- working conditions
- status
- and impact of work on home life.

To take a simple example, if the coffee machine does not work staff will become dissatisfied. Making it work will not motivate them to make greater efforts but it may restore a sense of contentment. At a more serious level people can be demotivated by real or imagined reductions in perceived status, regular late working which causes trouble at home or – one of the worst situations – wages being paid late.

Employees' needs

Yet another part of the jigsaw was completed by Abraham Maslow who developed the theory that workers are influenced by a 'hierarchy of needs'. This theory appeared in Maslow's book *Motivation and Personality* (published by Harper and Row in 1970).

The needs which Maslow identified start from some fairly obvious and basic human requirements (such as the need for food) and climb up a hierarchy to more sophisticated and less obvious demands. This hierarchy is illustrated in Figure 8.1. Levels 3 to 5 have significant implications for managers wishing to retain the willing services of their employees.

Maslow's hierarchy of needs

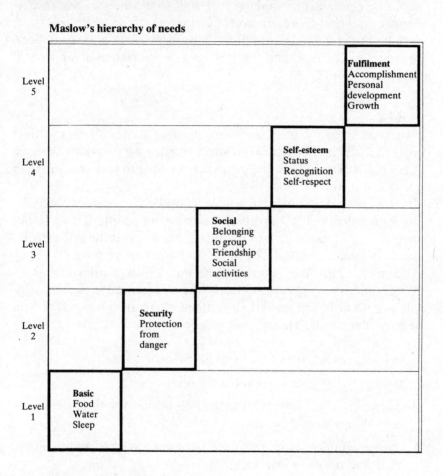

Level 3 – Social needs
In a working environment, social needs are fulfilled by a sense of belonging to the group or team, having friendships within the group and enjoying social activity with work colleagues. You can start to meet these needs by means of a proper induction scheme (as described in Chapter 6, page 80). The new employee, having been properly introduced into the working group, will have a greater sense of belonging and at an earlier stage than if this process is left to chance.

The manager also needs to recognise and resolve conflicts promptly and effectively. Many managers are reluctant to deal with conflict – a task which is often tricky and unpleasant. However, if not dealt with, it is likely to smoulder on and get worse. One way of avoiding conflict is by making sure that everyone's role is clearly defined and that there are no gaps or overlapping activities.

Finally, you need to adopt as many as possible of the practices recommended by Likert for the group management approach described on page 122.

Level 4 – Self-esteem.

Everyone from the most humble employee to the chief executive likes to feel 'important'. Self-respect and a sense that one's work is recognised are vital requirements for wishing to stay in a job and for doing it well.

It is often argued that recognising and giving status to people doing humdrum jobs is so difficult as to be impossible. This is by no means true – indeed it is sometimes easier to meet the self-esteem needs of junior staff than of those at the executive level.

Junior levels – including machine-minders, tea ladies, cleaners, filing clerks and general labourers – are all essential to the business and are no different from their more senior colleagues in terms of self-esteem needs. Their needs can be met by:

- treating them with courtesy at all times.
- saying 'thank you' for a job well done.
- discussing their jobs with them and asking for their views on how things should be done.
- encouraging other more senior people to treat them as colleagues and never as inferiors.
- keeping them informed of objectives, results of work done and what is going on.
- giving them as much freedom as possible to use their initiative and to make decisions about their own work.
- listening to them and taking the trouble to understand their problems.
- ensuring that they are fully aware of the importance of the work they do and how it fits in to the general scheme of things.

- providing opportunities for development and progress (including training), using skills to the full and giving real opportunities for increased responsibility.

The symptoms of failure to provide the necessary self-esteem factors include aggressive behaviour as a result of a sense of frustration and disappointment. Other symptoms to watch for are apathy and indifference, over-reaction to minor problems and difficulties, marked resistance to change and high absenteeism. These symptoms can appear at any level of the hierarchy. In this sense, senior people are no different from their junior colleagues.

Level 5 – Fulfilment

At once the most difficult to define and the most highly motivating, fulfilment is the highest on Maslow's scale of human needs. Fulfilment comes from a sense of achievement or accomplishment. It can result from having a painting accepted by the Royal Academy – and inspire another, better, painting. It can arise from successfully designing a new product – and inspire even greater effort and imagination to design yet another product.

Fulfilment can also be gained by more mundane achievements such as reaching trial balance in one go, ending a year with no errors in the invoices produced, or designing and implementing a new filing system which works.

A recently promoted filing supervisor said to his boss:

> This is what I have worked for. It may not seem much to you but this means a lot to me. What I want now is to run the best filing service we have ever had.

These comments expressed the supervisor's fulfilment needs. His boss's responsibility was to provide him with the opportunity and environment in which he could realise his ambition of having the best ever filing service. Helping the supervisor to satisfy his needs will stimulate his enthusiasm and loyalty. Failing to help – or placing obstacles in his way – will have the reverse effect, with all the symptoms of dissatisfaction listed earlier (on pages 120–1).

In this particular (real-life) case, the manager supported the supervisor by sending him on a short course on supervisory skills, agreeing objectives and standards with him and then delegating responsibility and authority to him. The supervisor rose to the occasion, as people normally do, and improved the filing service out of all recognition. The filing system was ultimately converted into a microfilm-based operation which in turn set new fulfilment targets for the supervisor. The formula was repeated – training in microfilm systems and equipment, new objectives and delegated powers. The supervisor retired, a happy man, when the task was completed some three years later.

One of the features of this case was delegation. This is a powerful motivator which improves the chances of the individual satisfying both self-esteem and fulfilment needs. However delegation is not just a matter of handing over a job or responsibility to someone else. The 'dump it on Charlie' approach can be a formula for disaster. The professional way to handle delegation is described on page 173.

A further essential requirement is communication. Unfortunately too many managers believe that communication needs are met by 'telling them what I want them to do'. This is far from the truth. The essentials of good communication and some ways to go about it are described in Appendix 3 (see page 177).

Meeting the needs

Although individual managers can do a great deal to meet the needs of their employees, a company policy is needed to create a culture for success. This should not be a mere form of words drafted in the board room and promptly forgotten. The overall boss must believe it and become personally involved in seeing that the policy is implemented.

Management objectives

The policy will be most effective if it is expressed in the form of management objectives, each of which must be followed by an action plan. Possible objectives could include:

- to establish a common sense of purpose throughout the company and to judge success by means of an appraisal scheme.

- to improve service to customers to a level where complaints arise in no more than 1 in 5,000 transactions.

- to raise staff enthusiasm for the company, its products and their jobs to a level where controllable resignations are below 5 per cent per annum.

- to recognise the need for change and to manage it in a positive way to the extent that at least 95 per cent of innovation is achieved on time.

As you can see, wherever possible the suggested objectives are expressed in a mathematical form. This is to ensure that results can be measured. It is not good enough to say, for instance, that staff enthusiasm should be improved. On its own, this is an almost meaningless statement which could be said to be satisfied when the chairman spots an employee smiling at 9 a.m. on a rainy Monday morning. Apart from controllable resignations, possible measures of staff enthusiasm are absenteeism rates (e.g. one-day sickness absence – which often occurs on Fridays or Mondays) and punctuality.

Achieving the objectives

Having set the objectives, we must now deal with how to achieve them. The first stage is to communicate the policy objectives to *all* staff – in terms that can be easily understood. The policy statement should be written and communicated in English and not some form of pseudo management science jargon. For example, you should avoid the following:

> It is the intention of management that the company will be pre-eminent in the market place, provide a service to customers in an environment of low fault ratio, and establish an ethos conducive to the personal fulfilment and satisfaction of the workforce.

A statement such as this will invite a two-word comment from the shop floor and not much more.

A series of simple statements such as 'We want to be the best in the industry', or, 'We will do everything we can to make working for the company enjoyable and not just a way to earn a living' can at least be understood. They may not be entirely believed at first and, if not, it is a demonstration that a lot of improvement is possible and necessary.

The next stage is to communicate to the managers and supervisors what is expected of them and the standards to which they should work. This can include:

- full and detailed attention to an induction scheme for new employees.

- all employees to have a job description, to know what is expected of them and the importance of their work.

- a training/development plan to exist for every employee.

- tasks and objectives to be set for both groups and individuals. The manager to consult with employees in setting objectives.

- arrangements for employees to monitor their own performances as far as possible.

- work to be planned and plans to be discussed with employees.

- decision, authority, responsibility and duties to be delegated as far down the line as possible in a controlled and constructive way.

- care to be taken of the personal well-being of every employee. Work conditions to be improved whenever and wherever possible, grievances to be promptly attended to and safety standards maintained at a very high level.

- recognition to be given to groups and individuals for achievements such as meeting targets, successfully implementing improved systems or reducing wastage.

- encouraging staff to express ideas and wherever possible allowing staff to implement them.

Putting these requirements into practice cannot be done successfully in a cold, clinical way. The atmosphere, for which the manager is responsible, should be warm, friendly and helpful. And much will depend on the manager himself. Ideally, he will project a cheerful and enthusiastic manner and avoid fussing about points of detail (e.g. splitting hairs and imposing petty rules and restrictions). He should constantly seek new ideas, have the courage to take tough decisions but always be seen as fair. A good manager will avoid pointless confrontations, be patient, sympathetic and prepared to see the funny side of situations (including being willing to laugh at himself). Perhaps most important, he will be able to admit his own mistakes and say to an employee, 'Sorry, Clara. You were right and I was wrong.'

All this is a very tall order – but good management is not easy and requires endless effort and practice. The manager will know when he is succeeding. The results will include:

- staff willing to report bad as well as good news – often with a ready-made solution to a problem.
- high levels of performance as a norm.
- staff co-operation and concern about problems.
- staff willingness to take on additional responsibility or work – including the dirty jobs.
- staff smile more often than they scowl.
- staff turnover and absenteeism are low.

Walking the job

The results listed above are unlikely to be achieved by a combination of good intentions and sitting on one's backside. The manager who sits in his office all day will never be fully aware of how things are going. Some managers are content to receive written reports and computer printouts, assuming that by reading them they are successfully monitoring activities. To some extent this may be true but it is likely to give the manager only a partial picture and it also means that he misses a great opportunity.

For the manager who really wants to know what is going on *and* to be in a position to lead his company or department, personal contact is the only solution. This means seeing and being seen by *everyone*, not just a few section leaders or supervisors who may be only too eager to act as a buffer between the boss and the sharp end. 'Walking the job' is an ideal way to gain people's commitment, to head off problems, to monitor morale and to see personally that everything is going to plan. You may find the following procedure helpful:

- allocate periods of time in your diary for walking the job. Since this is a priority, the allocated time should be regarded as inviolate. (A sudden heart attack might be allowed to stand in the way – but not much else.)

- go to the chosen department, section or whatever at the appointed time. Tell the person in charge that you are walking the job and give him the option of joining you. If he declines it is a very good sign. If he joins you it is not necessarily a bad sign!

- walk round from place to place and ask people about their jobs (e.g. what work they are doing, their views on the work and how they think things are going in general). Questions should be of the open variety and put in a friendly, casual way to encourage

131

informative answers. Use names wherever possible. (Ideally you will know the name of everyone you meet. If not, ask but don't pretend you know if you don't. Once they've told you, *remember*.)

- listen carefully to what people say and don't say. If you receive a complaint listen to it. If you can sort out the complaint on the spot then do so. If not, promise to look into it. Having looked into it, go back to the individual concerned and tell him the result personally. Naturally the individual's immediate boss must be involved to demonstrate that you are not usurping his position.

- get to know about people individually and, if they welcome it, discuss their interests with them. It is not a waste of time to spend a few minutes chatting about someone's success in a local charity fun run or the joys of becoming a grandparent. These are the things that matter to people.

- look at people's work and give praise and encouragement when appropriate.

- find out what people think about company policy or decisions taken further up the organisation. If there are misunderstandings take the time to explain why decisions have been taken and be prepared to listen to critical comment. Remember it is the employee's perception which will dominate his actions, not yours.

- discuss performance measured against targets in a constructive way. Show your interest in group and individual performance.

- check the working conditions, including cleanliness, ventilation, first aid facilities and toilet provisions. If you find something unsatisfactory do something about it.

When walking the job do avoid making it into a fault-finding expedition. Any idiot can find faults if he looks hard enough but it takes a manager to use the walkabout in a constructive and productive way. If you do find a fault don't throw your weight about. Tell the head of the department (not the individual employee) in private. Then make sure that the head of department 'discovers the fault himself' – and deals with it tactfully and constructively. If, after your visit, a number of employees are given a rocket for faults you have discovered there will be no point in walking the job any more.

Most of the time should be spent looking and listening. You can learn more in half an hour listening to the people on the shop floor than from a mountain of reports or hours of comment from intermediaries. In addition, although you may not make much impression during the first visit, or even the second, eventually the employees will realise that *you care* and *they matter*. Both will encourage them to stay with you.

Recognition and stress

Stress can make people ill and can often lead to them leaving for more congenial surroundings. Recent research in the USA has shown that stress can be reduced by praise and recognition. The emphasis of management should therefore be away from punishment when things go wrong to praise and recognition when things go right. The director of human resources at Xerox Corporation, writing in the magazine *Healthy Companies*, stated:

> Recognition is an important way to confirm a sense of personal accomplishment that, in turn, reduces counter-productive feelings of anxiety and stress.

As a result of this view, Xerox have introduced a 'recognition system' in which an employee who does particularly well is rewarded with a certificate which is redeemable for $25.

A number of hotel companies have 'employee of the month' schemes in which photographs of the winners are publicly displayed. Some of these schemes also involve some tangible reward such as meal vouchers, or bottles of champagne. In most cases the value of the tangible reward is low but as Professor Gary Cooper (of Manchester School of Management) said in an article in *The Sunday Times* (4 December 1988): 'Work is about feeling valued as well as about earning an income.'

Implementing change

The world is continually changing and business must change with it. New products introduced by competitors, new technology and even changes in Government can all make it necessary for an individual company to make changes.

Change is rarely welcome – we all tend to prefer the comfort of the status quo – and upheaval can cause people to become unsettled and look for a new job in disgust. This is another reason for adopting the right management style and method and developing a culture which treats change in a positive way. Rensis Likert said in *The Human Organisation*:

> The motivation of the members of an organisation can be crucial in determining whether labour-saving processes – computers or automated equipment – are made to work well or poorly. Supervisory and non-supervisory employees, if they wish to do so, can make excellent equipment perform unsatisfactorily and with frequent failures. These employees can also, if they desire to do so, rapidly eliminate the inadequacies in new processes or equipment and have the operation running smoothly in a surprisingly short time.

The accuracy of this statement has been demonstrated many times. It shows that good management will not only retain the services of your good people, it will also help them overcome the problem of change (and most other problems).

Dos and don'ts of keeping staff

- **do** measure the size of the problem by checking the facts surrounding resignation and monitoring 'wastage' figures on a regular basis.

- **do** look for pockets of unsatisfactory turnover which may be hidden in the overall figures (e.g. among female employees).

- **don't** make excuses for losing good staff. If someone goes and you are sorry about it then something went wrong.

- **do** look at the causes of resignation from the employee's viewpoint, not just your own.

- **don't** imagine that you cannot achieve the standards demanded by Likert's fourth style of management – you can.

- **do** remember the factors which Herzberg found can cause dissatisfaction if you get them wrong. **Don't** imagine that staff will be motivated if you get them right – the best you can expect is contentment.

- **do** recognise the human needs identified by Maslow and **don't** make the mistake of assuming that they only apply to *some* of your employees. They apply to everyone.

- **do** watch out for the signs that self-esteem needs are not being met.

- **do** provide opportunities for self-fulfilment. It is not necessarily difficult.*

- **do** learn how to delegate.

- **do** learn how to communicate.

- **do** establish policy objectives to create a company culture which encourages enthusiasm and commitment.

- **do** walk the job. It is time well spent.

* See also the section on Appraisals in Chapter 10.

9

ABSENTEEISM

ABSENTEEISM is, in effect, a form of temporary resignation – the difference being that in many cases the absent employee is still paid. Keeping absenteeism to a minimum is therefore perhaps even more important than keeping resignation to a minimum. The disruptive effects of absenteeism are often serious and can include:

- production losses
- sales losses and damage to company reputation (e.g. there is no one there to give the customer the service he wants)
- extra overtime, at premium rates, to compensate for the lack of manpower
- sudden, additional burdens on other employees who may be quite busy enough already
- delayed invoicing, adversely affecting cash flow
- and broken promises to employees, suppliers, tax authorities and anyone else the company deals with.

A simple example is the paper boy who fails to turn up in the morning. His boss, trying to keep his corner newsagency going, may decide to abandon the delivery service for the day, thereby losing sales and annoying his customers. Alternatively, he may close the shop to make the deliveries himself, thus losing customers for his other sales. Or he could send his assistant out on the paper round, leaving himself short-handed and possibly upsetting his assistant.

The same damaging effects will occur on a larger scale when, say, salesmen, van drivers, machine operators, clerical staff and so on are unexpectedly absent. And the damage also extends to additional pressure on supervisors and managers who suddenly have to juggle with resources to keep things going and meet deadlines. It is therefore important to gain an understanding of absenteeism, what it is, why it occurs and what can be done about it.

Defining absenteeism

Definitions of absenteeism vary from one company to another. Some keep records of absenteeism which include annual holidays, sanctioned training courses and jury service. Others are only concerned with absences which are unplanned and not sanctioned.

This chapter looks at absences resulting from sickness (genuine or otherwise) and other unpredictable short absences, whether or not the employer 'sanctions' them at any stage. These are the type of absences which are most likely to disrupt work schedules. They are also the ones most likely to include dubious and mysterious 'back pains' and sundry domestic emergencies.

Of course there are cases of long-term absence for dubious reasons – often depending on the arrangements for sick pay. A senior clerk in a London company went sick with a 'nervous complaint'. She regularly sent doctors' certificates to her employers confirming her illness. The company operated a scheme whereby during the first six weeks of absence the employee received full pay minus the state sickness benefit.

After six weeks payment was on a discretionary basis. The clerk continued to receive full pay after the six weeks but when the period of absence had lengthened to three months the employer's patience and sympathy had worn thin. A letter was sent to the employee stating that further payment would depend on an independent medical examination carried out by the company's doctor. The employee made a rapid, if not amazing, recovery and was back at work the day after receiving the letter.

However by no means all sickness absence is suspect – not even a regular Friday flu or monthly migraine. Some of these fairly intangible and/or unprovable illnesses are absolutely genuine even if the symptoms disappear with lightning speed on Saturday morning or by midday on a Monday. The causes of this type of illness are frequently related to management methods and will be discussed later in this chapter (see page 141).

Perhaps one of the most common concerns that employers have is what level of absenteeism to regard as 'normal' – they often ask, 'We have X per cent absenteeism. Is this good or bad?' As with turnover, one could say that any level above 0 per cent is bad, and in a sense that is true. However it is unrealistic to suppose that no one will ever be genuinely sick, malingering, dashing to the death bed of a close relative or whatever.

Absenteeism variation

In order to set your own standard or target you need some idea of what is to be expected. In fact absenteeism varies in a number of ways.

Variation from place to place

A survey of sickness absence among manual workers carried out in the UK and published in 1974 by the Department of Health and Social Security showed marked regional differences, with the worst area (Wales) exhibiting twice the national average rate. The figures were:

Area	Sickness days per person per year
Wales	32.2
North	25.3
Yorkshire	21.5
North-west	21
Scotland	20
South-west	16
East Midlands	15.9
West Midlands	14.9
East Anglia	12.9
South-east	10.5

Why the regional differences (as recorded in 1973) were so great is open to speculation. It seems unlikely that the people of Wales are markedly different in terms of basic human nature from people living in South-east England, yet their absence rates were three times as great.

A more recent survey carried out in 1987 by the Confederation of British Industry (CBI) showed that the North-west had the highest manual worker losses for reasons other than strikes and the South-west the lowest. For non-manual jobs the eastern region was worst and *Wales* the best. Since Wales had the worst score in the 1974 survey either things had improved overall by 1987 or the Welsh non-manual workers had a far better record than their manual colleagues.

Interpreting the statistics produced over the years by various enquiries is fraught with problems. Comparisons are difficult due to differences in definition and sampling method. However, according to the 1987 CBI survey, the average percentage of time lost is 4 per cent for manual workers and 2.2 per cent for non-manual workers. These figures provide a useful benchmark.

On a company level absenteeism is often found to vary markedly from department to department. It is often the case that total absences in a company conform to the 80:20 rule. This means that 80 per cent of the time lost is accounted for by only 20 per cent of the employees – or some similar ratio. And these high absence employees may well be concentrated in one or two departments.

The reasons for this concentration may be many, including an established or traditional department 'norm', the nature of the work and the quality of the supervision. It is unlikely that any particular group of people will be more prone to illness than another, assuming that none is doing work which positively encourages illness. Indeed Dr P. J. Taylor, writing in the Industrial Society's *Notes for Managers* (No. 15) states:

> A man's state of health is usually but one of the factors that decides whether or not he attends for work and, indeed, when he will consult a doctor.

Variation from time to time

Statistics show that sickness absence is higher in the winter months and, in the UK, concentrated in the first quarter of the year. According to Gary Roberts, the author of *Absent from Work* (Duncan Publishing, 1982), the favourite day for absence is Monday. These two features of absenteeism are to be found in different countries, industries and types of job.

The Industrial Society in its *Notes for Managers* (No. 15) mentions season and the state of the economy among the factors which affect sickness absence. It is not immediately clear why the state of the economy, as opposed to any other reason, should influence sickness absence in particular. There is some evidence that absenteeism in general tends to be high in depressed areas and poor social conditions may encourage sickness absence related to human depression and general despair. The state of the economy will vary from time to time both in national and regional terms and this could have an influence on the absence rates for individual businesses.

Variation from job to job

The General Household survey carried out in the UK in 1972 reported the following absence figures by broad types of job:

Type of job	Percentage of time lost
Professional workers	2.1
Managers	3.9
Junior non-manual	6
Skilled manual	7.5
Unskilled manual	7.9

These figures include absences for illness, accidents and other personal reasons but exclude holidays.

One might expect manual workers to be more prone to accidents than non-manual workers but there is no non-empirical evidence to explain why sickness rates should be any different. The figures imply that there is some other factor intrinsic to the type of work which determines absence levels.

Modern thinking favours the view that absence levels are universally proportional to levels of job satisfaction. This might well explain the substantial difference between the 2.1 per cent absence rate for professional workers and the 7.9 per cent rate for the unskilled manual workers. The chance of job satisfaction and a sense of achievement is clearly far greater for an architect, lawyer or accountant than it is for someone whose life is spent digging holes in the road or sweeping a factory floor. The fact remains – whatever the cause – that manual workers exhibit higher absenteeism rates.

The 1987 CBI survey also revealed that a substantial number of the companies involved in the study believed that 'non-attendance' was concentrated in certain individuals, groups or types. The people most frequently cited as making the greatest contribution to absenteeism were manual employees (especially female), young employees (including apprentices) and people close to retirement.

Possible explanations (which should be treated with caution) include the ideas that female employees are less interested than males in a career and treat their jobs less seriously, that young people adopt a less responsible attitude to work and that people close to retirement have nothing to lose by taking time off as their careers are over. Individual cases can no doubt be found to support these views but, like many generalisations, they would be danger-ous to use as a basis for a policy.

The causes of absenteeism

A secretary in an American chemical company was well known for her good work. She was in every respect, but one, a model employee. The one area of dissatisfaction was the frequency with which she would telephone her boss to say that either she would be very late or not come in at all. The reason, which her boss finally prised out of her, was that as part of a complicated family situation she was responsible for an aged and bedridden mother.

The secretary had to wash and feed her mother prior to leaving for work and had to make arrangements for her to be looked after during the day. From time to time the mother would be ill and/or there was no one available to attend to the old lady while the secretary was away from the house. The problem was resolved by allowing the secretary to work to flexitime and by the company using its influence with the local authority to provide day-care facilities for her mother. Such personal circumstances can be the cause of absenteeism – and the reason why it is concentrated in a few individuals.

The journey to work can also present problems, as London commuters are only too well aware. Having to live outside big cities in order to be able to find or afford housing, and the conse-quent journey to work, can give rise to absenteeism. Obviously this factor can be checked out before employing someone, but the problem can begin long after they are taken on when, for whatever reason, they move house.

There are also a number of more general causes to be considered. The CBI report quoted the views of the 343 companies surveyed and the following are the figures showing the percentage of companies citing a cause:

Cause	Manual workers	Non-manual
Work-related stress	16.6	32.8
Poor motivation	46.3	27.7
Drink-related	25	9.2
Domestic	44.6	38.7
Unauthorised extension to holidays	22.9	28.6

Various companies also mentioned moonlighting, and taking paid sick leave 'as of right' as causes. The paid sick leave cause is an interesting one. In companies which allow a certain number of days sickness per year to be paid absence one employee may say to another, 'Take a day off sick. You are *entitled* to it.' This attitude can result from cynical exploitation of the company but it can also be brought about by poor communication.

Another interesting cause mentioned in the CBI report was that of workers taking time off in order to make it necessary for them to work at weekends to make up the lost time and production. The weekend work would, of course, be paid at overtime rates. A variation on this theme could be seen at a warehouse in South Wales where work always slowed down on Fridays. Fork-lift trucks suddenly 'broke down', documents were 'lost' and other delaying phenomena cropped up. The result was that some of the despatches had to be completed on Saturdays. There was an agreement with the union that any period of work on Saturdays, however short, entitled the worker to a full day's pay at premium rates. It was not surprising that the Friday go-slow was a regular occurrence, as was some absenteeism on that day.

While some causes, such as moonlighting and manipulating the overtime rules, are both explicable and observable, two of the causes listed in the CBI report need some examination.

Stress

Of the companies surveyed, 32.8 per cent mentioned work-related stress in relation to non-manual workers while only 16.6 per cent mentioned it in relation to manual workers. Unless the CBI respondents carried out some kind of objective study before reporting, they may simply have been repeating a myth. This is the myth that 'executives' suffer stress and 'workers' do not. Such evidence as exists suggests that the reverse is more likely to be true.

In *Fit for Business* (published by Mercury, 1988) Matthew Archer refers to a University of Manchester study which showed that miners and policemen have the most stressful jobs. Top executives come some way down the list. Archer points out that stress is not the same as pressure – indeed lack of pressure can be stressful for some people. He argues that a boss who is indecisive, stupid or lazy, unappreciative, unhelpful or over-authoritarian will cause stress by causing frustration. In such cases it is the subordinate who suffers stress, and since the bulk of manual workers are subordinates that is where the stress will lie. It is also self-evident that non-manual workers have far more opportunity to gain real satisfaction and emotional reward from their jobs and the more senior the job the greater the opportunity.

It is the quality of management and supervision – or lack of it – which may account for the Monday morning migraine mentioned earlier. The employee waking up on Monday to face another week working for a boss with the personality of a bad-tempered boa constrictor and all the sensitivity of a frightened buffalo *needs* a migraine – it is the lesser of the two evils. A company doctor familiar with the Monday morning absence syndrome reckoned that most of them were genuine but psychosomatic. He also stated that he could often tell which boss the people concerned worked for. Most of the regulars worked in one department notorious for its martinet of a boss – who retired early for reasons of mental ill-health.

This opinion on the link between illness and the working atmosphere is by no means new. In the 1930s Ronald Ross, a British psychiatrist, pointed out that illness and absence from work were both modes of behaviour which characterised an unhappy person.

Motivation

There is no doubt that many manual workers lack motivation and again the CBI figures are higher for them than for non-manual workers. If the figures are in any way representative of the true state of affairs then the managements concerned clearly have a great deal of work to do. Motivation is a prime responsibility of management and it is no use merely stating that the workers are not motivated as if it is all their fault!

The same applies to those companies who cited lack of motivation as a cause of absenteeism in non-manual workers. If the motivation is not there the management must provide it.

Reducing absenteeism

The first step in dealing with absenteeism is a policy which is clearly communicated to the whole workforce. The content of the policy will vary from company to company depending on a variety of circumstances, including company and industry traditions, the nature of the business and 'the mix' of employees, the type of work done, the attitudes of management, the location, and the working hours and conditions.

For example, the policy required for a law firm in London's West End employing 50 people may be very different from the policy for a light engineering business employing 250 people on an industrial estate. Very different circumstances would also apply in a private hospital, an airport, on a farm or in a school. However most policies would include clear statements on the following:

- the levels of absence which will be accepted before enquiry leading to possible disciplinary action results.
- requirements for supervisors and managers to keep records and take action.
- the obligations of employees, e.g. telephoning when absent, provision of sick notes, etc.
- effect of absences on pay and promotion.
- company assistance to employees faced with personal problems likely to result in absence.
- reasons for absence which will be tolerated and reasons which will not.
- level and frequency of absence which the company will accept for the purposes of studying and taking examinations, and which subjects of study will receive company support.

Once decided, the policy must be translated into action by organising the appropriate procedures. For example, supervisors may be required to keep records of absences and to notify a more senior person when any individual exceeds a given level of absence. The procedure for self-certification should also be made clear and arrangements for obtaining a second medical opinion when required.

The CBI report recorded the following factors or measures which responding companies recognised or used to reduce absenteeism. The figures against each item are the percentage of companies quoting them:

Measure used	Manual workers	Non-manual
Fear of redundancy	35	33
Peer group pressure	18	27
Improved motivation	17	25
Improved monitoring	70	59
Attendance bonuses	8	2
Profit/incentive schemes	15	7
Flexible hours	13	15

The first two factors are not created by management – although both fear and peer group pressure can be stimulated. The remaining items are all measures which management can take. A high standard of monitoring is a clear favourite for all types of employee – a process which might be less in demand if more attention were paid to motivation. Unfortunately motivation falls far short of improved monitoring in perceived effectiveness.

Attendance bonuses have been used from time to time over many years. The argument against them is that, providing every employee is paid a fair wage for the job, there should be no need to bribe them with extra cash to turn up. The counter-argument is an economic one. If the attendance bonus produces results, and costs less than the absence it has prevented, it is a good investment. The problem is proving what the absence level would have been if the bonus system had not been in existence.

Bonuses came into the news in 1989 when British Rail announced a scheme whereby certain employees in regions of staff shortage would receive additional pay subject to performance *and* attendance. The rules provided for cancellation of a week's bonus as a result of a one-day absence. The union representing the staff immediately announced their opposition to the scheme on the grounds that the scheme 'undermines the concept that shift working is a national phenomenon which is rewarded equally, irrespective of geographical location'. The union stated their clear preference for a 'realistic basic rate of pay' with, presumably, no incentive to stop taking days off.

Flexible working hours might, in future, be more widely recognised as a measure of reducing absenteeism. The advantage of flexitime is that it gives employees some latitude so that they can deal with personal matters during normal business hours (e.g. seeing a solicitor or bank manager) without taking a whole day off to do it. If there is no flexitime the employee may lose money or fear getting into trouble if he sees the bank manager and then arrives late at work. The temptation in such cases is to take the whole day off and report sick. Flexitime also allows an employee to accumulate time until a whole day can be taken legitimately when it is needed.

Other measures

The Advisory Conciliation and Arbitration Service (ACAS) publishes a booklet in which it makes recommendations for reducing absenteeism. These include:

- good working conditions
- rigorously maintained health and safety standards
- adequate training for new starters – especially young people
- policies and work designed to create job satisfaction
- adequate supervisor training
- flexitime
- crèches
- special leave provision for such needs as bereavement, religious observance and ante-natal care
- careful monitoring of absence records
- a requirement to telephone in
- supervisors to talk to employees regarding all absences
- and a rule concerning absences occurring immediately before or after official holidays.

The Industrial Society recommends that companies should aim to maximise job satisfaction as a means of reducing absenteeism. Among other things it suggests:

- an atmosphere in which serious discussion with the individual about his job can take place.
- concentrated analysis in the areas or departments where the need is greatest.
- some aspect of each individual's job that allows him to make decisions.
- work organised so that the individual can obtain support and assistance from colleagues.
- some recognisable status for each job.
- the individual should know what his job is and how he is performing.

These recommendations for reducing absenteeism are very similar to those in Chapter 8 for keeping people in the company. Fortunately for managers, achieving one objective will simultaneously result in success in the other.

The Industrial Society also suggests that a study should be made of the small proportion of employees who regularly take time off and the small proportion who never take time off. The analysis, it is suggested, can indicate how working hours, conditions, incentives or supervision might be improved.

Another idea which has worked well in the USA and is slowly spreading to other countries is the establishment of a company-backed fitness scheme. In *Fit for Business* Matthew Archer quotes the case of a Canadian company which reduced absenteeism by 42 per cent by means of a fitness programme. An American company achieved a 55 per cent reduction in sickness absence with a similar scheme and another found that those on a scheme averaged losses of 3.5 days per year against 8.6 days per year for employees not on the scheme.

Anything a company can do to promote fitness could have profitable results *and* generally improve morale. Usually only the large companies can offer playing fields, tennis courts, squash courts and the like. But smaller companies could consider:

- subsidising membership fees for local sports clubs and centres.
- booking time at local squash courts or bowling alleys and setting up a league for employees.
- organising clubs for jogging, cycling, swimming or other activities which either require no special facilities or facilities that can be hired.

Competitions with worthwhile prizes could be an incentive for employees to take part in any activity which the company organises. Whatever the circumstances, the importance of absenteeism in terms of profit lost should never be overlooked.

Dos and don'ts of absenteeism

- **do** recognise the cost of absenteeism and the importance of paying attention to it. Absenteeism is a form of temporary resignation which you pay for.

- **don't** automatically assume that the Friday flu or Monday migraine absences are fake. The illness could be genuine even if the symptoms disappear rapidly. It could be a real illness caused by poor management.

- **do** keep records of absenteeism. You will probably find that the majority of absences are accounted for by a minority of the people – or are concentrated in one area of the business. Once you know where it is you are better able to deal with it.

- **do** look closely at the causes of your absenteeism. **Don't** assume things or follow fashionable views. Stress, for instance, is *not* limited to executives – it is more likely to appear on the shop floor.

- **do** have a carefully thought-out policy (and procedures) for dealing with absence. **Do** make sure they are properly communicated to everyone.

- **do** select some methods (appropriate to your business) from those recommended and try them out. Measure the results.

10

WHAT TO DO IF THINGS TURN SOUR

HOWEVER good we are at selecting people – and getting them settled into the company – things can go wrong. It is not uncommon to find employees who work well for a long period and then suddenly or gradually become a problem. Sometimes, apparently inexplicably, industrious employees can become 'lazy', co-operative employees become unco-operative and hitherto careful workers produce sloppy work.

A natural reaction to such a situation may be to dismiss the employee – or to start a process of warnings leading to dismissal. But giving in to this reaction is not the best way to tackle the problem. Stern warnings can often make the employee's behaviour even worse. And the prospect of dismissal then becomes a costly reality.

The cost of dismissal

When an employee is recruited a considerable sum of money may have been spent on finding him. This will have been followed by a settling-in and training period during which further costs will have been incurred (including the low productivity which is normally associated with a newcomer learning the job). Although this money can never be recovered in cash terms it still amounts to an investment. And return on this investment is cut off as soon as the employee leaves the company. In addition, if it is necessary to replace a dismissed employee all the recruitment and settling-in costs must be repeated.

There is another, hidden, cost which can be considerable. This is the effect of a dismissal on other employees. It is a fact of human nature that when someone is on the way up in their career other

149

people will be jealous or resentful. When someone is on the way down there is a tendency to sympathise with them *even if their decline is fully justified*. In other words, a visibly poor performer suffering the consequences of his own actions is still likely to gain the support of colleagues when the axe falls. 'I know old George made a lot of mistakes but kicking him out was a bit rotten' is a common reaction when even a well-deserved dismissal takes place.

Every dismissal also has a disturbing effect on other employees' sense of security. 'Will I be next?' ask close colleagues. This problem is particularly difficult to deal with because warnings to employees – and the reasons for them – are not likely to be made public. The errant employee's colleagues will probably not know the full story and may well only hear the employee's version. This version is not likely to include the full justification for disciplinary action or any justification at all.

There are, then, more than enough reasons to treat dismissal and the steps leading up to it as a last resort. Fortunately there are many preventive and corrective actions which can be taken, to good and cost-saving effect. There are, though, some cases where losing the employee is inevitable and where preventive actions have only limited application.

When dismissal is inevitable

There are certain acts which the lawyers refer to as 'gross misconduct'. These can justify, both morally and legally, instant dismissal. This type of misconduct is described in the ACAS advisory handbook, *Discipline at Work*:

> Gross misconduct is generally seen as misconduct serious enough to destroy the employment contract between the employer and the employee and make any further working relationship and trust impossible. It is normally restricted to very serious offences – for example physical violence, theft or fraud – but may be determined by the business or other circumstances.

In addition to the offences mentioned by ACAS, dismissal could also be the penalty for drunkenness, wilful damage to property, taking illegal drugs or gambling on company premises.

There is *some* preventive action which can be taken.

Employees can be told in their contract of employment that those acts will result in instant dismissal. The knowledge of this may have a deterrent effect – and removes the excuse that the employee did not know. (Such an excuse could be offered to a tribunal or court if the employee sues the company for unfair dismissal.)

Prevention

An essential function of management is to get the best out of people. This requires continuous action rather than ad hoc reaction when something is going adrift.

Appraisal schemes

One 'tool' of management which, when properly applied, is effective in improving performance and encouraging stability (i.e. reducing resignations) is the appraisal scheme. (Refer also to Chapter 8).

Appraisals are not mere 'counselling' sessions, nor are they formal opportunities for the boss to tell the employee what his faults are. In the appraisal interview both parties can discuss the employee's performance and agree on constructive future action which will benefit *both* the company and the employee. During the interview the manager communicates his impression of the employee's performance. This is then discussed with a view to establishing an objective reflection of the employee's past performance which is acceptable to both parties, as well as a clearly understood and agreed set of objectives, performance standards and targets for the future.

The purpose of this is:

- to develop and motivate the employee in his present job and for future assignments.
- to let the employee know where he stands and what his manager thinks of his work.
- to help the employee to understand how he can improve himself and to identify how the company can help him, e.g. by additional training.
- to recognise good work – and let the employee know this.
- to assess the work of the department as a whole. The discussions

give the manager an insight into morale and 'feeling' in the department – and any action which should be taken.

The appraisal interview takes place in the context of the organisation. If the interview is to contribute to the company's policy on manpower and development, the manager must therefore keep in mind possible career patterns (i.e. those affected by company long-term policy) and organisational changes likely in the future.

Preparing for the interview

Preparation for the interview is important and the manager should make sure he advises the employee of the time and place of the interview – and explains its purpose (i.e. it is not a witch-hunt but a means to find ways to improve). He should allow *uninterrupted* time for the interview, familiarise himself with all the details of the employee and his job and be quite clear about the purpose of the interview himself. Most of all, he needs to consider his own attitudes towards the employee. He should try to be objective and not allow any personal feelings to cloud his judgement.

Conducting the interview

The interview should be conducted in ways somewhat similar to the recruitment interview. The manager should:

- open with a neutral remark.
- discuss achievements specifically.
- use open questions to obtain more expression of feelings, attitudes and motives.
- listen to what is said – *and* to what can't be said.
- avoid becoming emotionally involved, e.g. by defending himself or showing annoyance.
- adopt a neutral stance.
- put himself in the employee's place and see the situation from his point of view.
- try to work for agreement for the future.
- give opportunities for the employee to ask questions, make comments and suggestions for the future.

Ideally, the interview will end with full agreement on what is to be done in future as a result of a free and friendly discussion. The employee's aspirations, fears, worries, difficulties, complaints and opinions should have been well aired and taken into account. It is not unusual for a manager to discover, during appraisal, attitudes or problems which he was wholly unaware of and which, if not dealt with, could have led to deteriorating performance and disciplinary action.

The interview has the great benefit of providing an opportunity to get problems out in the open. This does not easily happen during the daily hustle and bustle when both manager and employee are too busy to get down to brass tacks for a sufficient length of time. There are also employees who will bottle up their unhappiness. The appraisal interview helps them to take the cap off the bottle.

The interview should be closed with a review of the points discussed and agreed on, and a written statement of the action to be taken.

After the interview

The result of a successful interview might be a programme, jointly agreed, such as the one below.

	Action needed	Reason	Action by	Timing
1.	Training in invoice preparation	Error complaints	Manager	By 1 March
2.	Provision of larger work surface	Problems in handling computer printouts	Manager	By 1 April
3.	Training in statistical technique at evening college	Potential promotion to section supervisor	Employee	Spring term
4.	Attendance at section supervisor's weekly meeting	To make work as acting supervisor easier when supervisor absent	Employee	Start with next meeting
5.	Further discussion	To check progress	Employee Manager	1 May

153

Much information can be gained by looking at the various actions and the reasons for them. The complaints about invoicing errors – a particularly unpleasant problem because it concerns both money and customers – could, if not attended to, result in a move towards dismissal. At the appraisal interview it is recognised that the employee's training was inadequate and this leads to training being provided. This action is far more constructive than merely grumbling at, or about the employee, without finding out the cause of the problem.

'Yes,' you may say, 'but surely it should not need an appraisal interview to sort out a problem such as this.' You would be right but in real life these problems do not always receive attention and the situation drags on without the remedy being applied. In effect, the appraisal interview says, 'Stop. What is going on? Let's find out what we need to do.'

The work surface is another problem. Handling 10 metres of computer printout is not easy on an ordinary small desk and the simple provision of a proper place to do it could remove a major annoyance which has been adversely affecting the employee's performance.

The training in statistical technique, which the employee himself must obtain, is recognition of his ambition to take on a more senior job and one of the prerequisites of promotion. The employee knows what he must do to qualify himself. No less important, it gives him something to work for.

Attending the section supervisors' meetings has the stated purpose of making it easier for the employee to stand in for his section supervisor. This will help to ease the burden of acting as supervisor but also gives him some added visible status. This will have a motivating effect, encouraging the employee to get the invoicing error problem sorted out and to press on with the statistical training.

Further discussions are a vital part of the plan drawn up at any appraisal interview. It is not unknown for an employee to be greatly pleased and encouraged by future plans, only to be thoroughly demotivated when the plans are not properly implemented. Such situations lead to deterioration of performance rather than improvement. It is the manager's job to follow up, ensuring that what was agreed is put into practice and checking that the results are those required.

Most companies which use appraisal schemes carry out a yearly interview. Some find that a twice-yearly interview is more effective – especially for younger employees. Whichever frequency is chosen, the appraisal should be regarded as an essential part of the manager's job and as deserving of time as any other part. It could well be a major way of preventing things turning sour.

Ad hoc preventive action

Whatever long-term arrangements the company may have, ad hoc action may still be needed from time to time. Immediate action can often nip a problem in the bud but its effectiveness largely depends on the way the action is taken. Some forms of action can make the situation worse and at least a few minutes thought are needed before the exasperated manager wades in. First and foremost, the manager should consider the circumstances.

For instance, is the unsatisfactory behaviour uncharacteristic of the person concerned? Perhaps the person has become rude and aggressive after months of tactful and diplomatic behaviour.

Have I got the facts right? There is nothing worse or potentially more damaging than blaming someone for something they did not do – or did with very good reason.

Is it *my* fault? Perhaps you failed to ensure that the employee knew what was expected of him, the standards required – or how to do the job at all.

Finally, were the circumstances unusual? The breakdown of the computer last month may have reduced the time available to do a job which depended on the output from the computer. Failure to meet a deadline under such circumstances may not indicate a sub-standard performance. The employee may in fact have worked long and hard but been unable to make up the time. Such a case hardly warrants a ticking off or a warning.

In fact there is very frequently a reason for poor performance which the sensitive manager can deal with one way or another without provoking a crisis. The first requirement is to talk to the errant employee, privately and calmly, to point out the apparent failure and identify the cause.

The employee's comments should be listened to carefully and if a satisfactory explanation is received the matter should be closed without further ado. The manager may find that he needs to make some effort to see that a similar situation does not arise again but as far as the employee is concerned the subject should be closed.

If no satisfactory explanation is received the manager must ensure that the employee fully understands what improvement is needed and that future performance will be monitored. He may also have to tell the employee that if there is no improvement formal disciplinary procedures will follow, possibly leading up to dismissal.

However, do remember that in such cases the cause may be something to do with the employee's private life. The possibilities include financial problems, ill-health of spouse, behaviour of children (e.g. drug-taking teenagers), marital disputes or housing problems. Such pressures on the individual can have a marked effect on work quality and quantity and sometimes lead to unco-operative attitudes and aggressiveness.

It is not always easy to discover these background causes and probing into an employee's private life may well be resented. However some people struggling with personal problems will welcome the chance to talk about them. If so, the manager at least knows what the root causes are. An enlightened employer will do everything possible to help in such cases, as this is good for the health of the business as well as the employee.

Some managers regard private life problems as the concern of the employee only and insist on good work and behaviour regardless. This attitude is short-sighted as the case of Humphrey (not his real name) illustrates. Humphrey was in his mid-40s and had been with his company for over 20 years. He had started as a junior clerk and had worked his way up to a fairly senior supervisor level. Although never regarded as a potential high flyer, Humphrey was respected as a hard worker who produced good work and was liked by his colleagues and subordinates.

Quite suddenly Humphrey changed. The quality of his work went down and he became morose and bad-tempered. After he made a fairly serious mistake his boss called him in and gave him 'a piece of his mind'. Things went from bad to worse and Humphrey had more tickings-off, but no one asked him *why* his performance was so poor and so out of character. After a number of warnings Humphrey was dismissed.

A few days later it was learned that Humphrey had committed suicide. Further enquiry revealed that about the time that his work began to deteriorate Humphrey's wife had left him for another man and his children had blamed him for this. Someone remarked at the time, 'If only we had asked Humphrey what was wrong we might have prevented his suicide.'

Fortunately problem situations are rarely as dramatic or tragic as Humphrey's case. Many causes of poor work or behaviour have simple, easily resolved causes. Managers should look out for:

- genuine grievances over pay, working conditions, holiday rotas and the like
- 'misunderstandings' which can cause frustration and resentment
- poor supervision
- status worries
- and real or imagined unfairness.

All these causes lie within the company and can normally be dealt with by the manager – some very easily. The most effective preventive measures are *anticipation* of problems likely to bring about unsatisfactory performance and some commonsense avoiding action.

Alternatives to dismissal

Dismissal is not the only course of action if discussion (and any subsequent action) fails to achieve the required result. In many cases dismissal may, in any event, have to be preceded by a lengthy and formal process of warnings before legal requirements are met. So, what can the employer do instead? A number of alternatives have been used in the past but none is wholly satisfactory.

Suspension

Suspension can be an illegal action, especially if pay is withheld. But suspension *with pay* is a useful measure in cases where the matter is serious and time is needed to ascertain the facts. Fighting or damage to company property may warrant paid suspension while investigations are carried out into who was to blame.

Demotion

The problem with demotion is that it also demotivates, leaving a disgruntled employee only too happy to influence others against the company. It is difficult to imagine any situation in which demotion is a good idea.

Transfer

Moving an employee to another job can be very helpful if it means moving a square peg from a round hole to a square one. Poor performance can result from an employee having work to do which is unsuited to his talents or personality. If an alternative job can be found the problem may be over. However moving the person for no clear reason merely shifts the problem elsewhere.

Fines

Fines rarely do anything but make the situation worse, and in many countries (including the UK) are likely to be illegal.

No salary increase

This method, sometimes chosen because it is legal, is wholly unconstructive and demotivating. The employee who is told that his salary will not be increased at the next review will not be encouraged to improve. This method is sometimes used as a means of encouraging an employee to resign quietly. Until he does, he is a potential threat to the company and his resentment can manifest itself in a number of damaging ways.

Fake redundancy

Telling the employee that he is redundant is one way of getting rid of him (at the cost of his redundancy pay entitlement) but it must be genuine redundancy. Employers have been known to pretend that an unsatisfactory employee is redundant as a 'comfortable' way of dismissing him. Not only is this a thoroughly weak and unethical approach, it also lays the employer open to well-deserved legal action if the employee realises that the redundancy was not genuine.

Constructive dismissal

This is the term used to describe those situations where the employer makes life so unbearable for the employee that he is virtually forced to resign. In effect, the employer deliberately breaches his contract with the employee by, for example, giving him work to do which is far below that which his qualifications and experience demand.

Such a case occurred in a company which took on a young man as a marketing specialist. The young man served out three months notice with his previous employers, by which time the new employer had changed his mind about what he wanted. The new man started the job, only to be given work suitable for an employee at a much lower level. After some protests he walked out, put the case in the hands of a lawyer and won.

Other variations on this theme are giving the unwanted employees all the dreariest or dirtiest work, putting them on unpopular shifts or even refusing car parking space. Such tactics, apart from their doubtful legality, are neither ethical nor commercially desirable. All the other employees can see what is going on!

Buying them off

This is a popular method of getting rid of unwanted senior executives – not always because their performance is unsatisfactory. However it is not restricted to the higher levels.

A British company, deciding that a whole department was performing badly, took the view that the best course was to dismiss them all without warning or notice but with three months pay. The director whose idea it was said, 'Three months pay takes years to save up. It is enough to guarantee they will go without fuss and it's cheap at the price.'

Not everyone would agree with these sentiments – including the courts – if an employee treated like that decided to sue.

'Look for another job'

This is a method which can work well and is in the interests of both employer and employee. It is normally most applicable to people looking for career opportunities who clearly will not find them where they are. It has the merit of being an honest approach and should follow strenuous efforts to put right the employee's inadequacies.

Having failed to achieve the desired result, the employer can put the proposal to the employee in the following terms:

'George, we both know that your performance is consistently unsatisfactory and we have discussed this with you several times. We have made every effort to help you improve but we have reached the stage where we would be entitled to take steps to dismiss you.

'However this would be bad for your record and we don't want to be hard on you. We suggest that you look for another job where you would have some prospect of success and promotion and we will give you reasonable time off for interviews.'

Naturally, this method would not be appropriate in every case (e.g. where the employee is a persistent trouble-maker) but it can be used when the employee has tried but failed. A time limit may have to be imposed or the process of looking for another job could be extended indefinitely.

Although the employee will not be motivated by this method he is unlikely to be disgruntled, and other employees will probably see the treatment of their colleague as humane and fair. People presented with this option, recognising that they are not likely to make any progress where they are, will normally accept it and leave in due course with no hard feelings.

Dismissal – the last resort

Having tried every reasonable way to correct the unsatisfactory employee, the time may come when dismissal is the only remaining option. It is important that the action taken is fair, seen to be fair, and within the law relating to dismissal.

Every company should have a clearly laid down disciplinary procedure which should be followed with care. To ensure that there is no breach of the law it is wise to consult a lawyer when drawing up the procedure. Small firms in the UK could use the following procedure:

Stage 1
The employee is given an oral warning of unsatisfactory conduct or performance and this warning is recorded. The warning will be disregarded after, say, three months' satisfactory service.

160

Stage 2
If there is no improvement within the period stated (or if the offence is particularly serious) a written warning is given. The warning will state that if there is no improvement within 3 months a final written warning will be given.

Stage 3
If there is no improvement a final written warning is given. This warning will state that if there is any recurrence within X months dismissal will follow.

Stage 4
If there is continued unsatisfactory performance or conduct the employee is dismissed.

The procedure should allow for the employee to state his case at every stage and, if he wishes, be represented by a union official or fellow employee. The employee should also have the right of appeal to a more senior level in the company.

Such a disciplinary procedure will be more effective if backed up by company rules. These indicate the type of conduct which will lead to dismissal – and conduct which will result in dismissal without notice. The rules should be clear, in writing, and prominently displayed and/or individually issued to each employee.

Notice periods

Depending on the employee's contract of employment, length of service and the reason for his dismissal, he may be entitled to a period of notice or payment in lieu. The payment in lieu option should be seriously considered and any feelings about losing more money on a 'bad' employee set aside. A dismissed employee serving out his notice is not likely to work well or even work at all. He is much more likely to be a source of trouble. In extreme cases he may even set out to damage your company and the longer he is around the more opportunity he has to do so.

It is not unknown, for example, for computer staff to place a 'bug' in your system so that some time after the employee has departed the computer will wipe out the sales ledger or produce a payroll with everyone's pay altered in some way. Sales office staff have been known to place fake orders in the system so that unwanted deliveries are made. In one case an employee under notice dumped company files in the River Thames on his way home!

The potential for damage is considerable and is best removed by getting the employee off the premises without delay and giving him a cheque to cover his notice period.

The law

Employers in the UK (and other Western countries) are faced with a whole mass of legislation to which they must conform and (in jurisdictions where case law is effective) the *interpretation* of the law by the courts.

The crux of UK law is that dismissal must be *reasonable*. The Court of Appeal in Dobie v. Burns International Security Services (UK) Ltd stated:

> A very important factor of which [the employer] has to take account, on the facts known to him at the time, is whether there will or will not be injustice to the employee and the extent of that injustice.

In Polkey v. A. E. Dayton Ltd (1987) the House of Lords clearly stated that the issue of fairness of a dismissal does not depend on whether the employee has been treated fairly but on whether the employer has acted reasonably. If there has been a failure to operate a disciplinary procedure this ruling operates in favour of the employee – even if there are ample grounds for dismissal.

Provided that a disciplinary procedure exists and is carefully followed with due respect for the employee's rights, most dismissal cases should be within the requirements of the law. However the details must be handled correctly as well and the employer must be aware of such aspects as statutory minimum notice periods, the rights of pregnant women, what the law regards as misconduct and how formal warnings should be worded. The main legal provisions which should be studied and understood are listed on page 199.

Dos and don'ts of correction and dismissal

- **don't** react to unsatisfactory conduct or work with an automatic move towards dismissal. Dismissal is expensive and it is better to find ways to rectify the situation.

- **do** build in some on-going preventive measures such as an appraisal scheme. Prevention is better, and cheaper, than cure.

- **do** use ad hoc opportunities, thoughtfully and constructively, to put matters right and prevent future trouble.

- **do** look for hidden reasons for unsatisfactory performance and conduct.

- **don't** use dubious methods such as fake redundancy as an alternative when dismissal is justified.

- **do** treat dismissal as a last resort. But if it is unavoidable **do** follow a pre-agreed procedure which will hold up later if the dismissed employee takes action against you.

- **do** familiarise yourself with the law and always behave 'reasonably'.

IF YOU WANT
TO KNOW MORE

===1===

McGREGOR'S X AND Y THEORY OF MANAGEMENT

IN *The Human Side of Enterprise* (published in 1960) Douglas McGregor put forward the view that there were traditional management attitudes to workers. These attitudes McGregor called theory X assumptions. The 'theory X manager' works according to the following assumptions:

- the average human being has an inherent dislike of work and will avoid it if he can.
- because of their dislike of work, most people must be controlled and threatened before they will work hard enough.
- the average human prefers to be directed, dislikes responsibility, is unambitious, and desires security above everything.

A substantial number of managers believe these statements to be true, as anyone who has been in business long enough to see them in action will confirm. Some people will have met them on their first day at work when their enthusiasm is killed off by a supervisor or foreman saying something like: 'Right, let's get it straight. You are here to work, not to mess about. I shall be keeping a close eye on you, young woman.' At a slightly more sophisticated level the statement might be: 'We expect a 110 per cent effort here. We have no room for passengers or people who fall short of corporate standards.'

McGregor argued that the X assumptions, which give rise to 'tough' management with threats, punishment and controls, are wholly inadequate. In particular, theory X managers do not give their staff the opportunity to gain fulfilment from their jobs. McGregor also argued that because of this lack of opportunity employees actually *do* behave in the expected fashion in a theory X environment.

The alternative, and more accurate, set of assumptions McGregor called theory Y. The theory Y assumptions are:

- the expenditure of physical and mental effort in work is as natural as play or rest.

- control and punishment are not the only ways to make people work – man will direct himself if he is committed to the aims of the organisation.

- if a job is satisfying the result will be commitment to the organisation.

- the average man learns, under proper conditions, not only to accept but to seek responsibility.

- imagination, creativity and ingenuity can be used to solve work problems by a large number of employees.

- under the conditions of modern industrial life the intellectual potentialities of the average man are only partially utilised.

McGregor could perhaps have added a statement to the effect that theory X managers actively discourage people from staying in the company. Examples can be readily found – particularly in retail, catering and hotel businesses where a number of branches are controlled from a central head office. These types of business are characterised by high turnover of staff, especially at junior levels, which can in turn have a devastating effect on customer service. The following are real life examples of theory X at work.

Case 1: Teach them a lesson

A business executive who regularly travelled to a provincial British town was pleased to find that a new, modern and comfortable hotel had recently opened. He began to use the hotel and, although there were obvious teething troubles, he appreciated the willingness of the staff. During his first few visits he found that the waitresses, receptionists and other staff were cheerful and helpful if, at times, in need of training and experience.

As the weeks went by the executive noticed a gradual deterioration in the atmosphere. The smiles were being replaced by scowls and the quality of service was rapidly declining. One evening, while eating in the hotel restaurant, he was approached by a waitress who asked him if he remembered having dined there the previous week. He said that he did remember and the waitress told him that he had left the restaurant without signing his bill and, as a result, had not been charged for his dinner on his final account. The waitress begged him to pay the missing amount – which had been deducted from her wages!

The executive, horrified that the waitress had been made to pay for his dinner, immediately settled the matter at the reception desk and asked for the amount to be reimbursed to the waitress. 'Only the manager has the authority to do that,' he was told.

The following day he spoke to the manager who stated his reluctance to reimburse the waitress because, 'We have to teach them a lesson.' The executive, angry at this attitude, declared that if the money was not repaid he would never stay at the hotel again and would ensure that no one else from his company stayed there either.

At this the manager began to whine and plead, explaining that he had many difficulties. Not the least of his problems was the shortage of good staff in the area. He explained that when they did find good people, they left as soon as they had been trained. In addition, it seemed, no amount of punishment would make them do their work properly and many of them had to be dismissed.

During a visit the following week, the executive found that the waitress had been paid her money, and had also resigned as soon as she received it.

Case 2: Squeezing them dry

A branch of a large retail chain experienced a very busy and demanding time in the run-up to Christmas. The manager and the staff had worked hard and a very creditable 15 per cent increase in sales over the previous year had been achieved.

By the day before Christmas Eve the staff were tired and feeling the strain. Late in the day the regional director appeared at the shop and made an inspection. He noted that many of the shelves were empty or nearly empty and complained strongly to the manager. The manager pointed out that sales were 15 per cent up on the previous year and that the staff were run off their feet. They had not had time to spare from serving customers to re-stock the shelves and, in any case, it was only to be expected that stock on display would be low by the end of the day.

The director was not impressed and told the manager that if the shelves were not full by the start of business on Christmas Eve his future was in jeopardy. The manager, lying, said that the staff were coming in at 7 a.m. the following morning to fill the shelves. The director, satisfied, departed with no word of congratulation on the sales performance or the efforts of the manager and his people. The manager had lied knowing that the staff were in need of a good rest and an early start the next day would be more than they could cope with. Instead, he and his supervisors filled the shelves during the night.

The manager explained that if he had ordered the staff in early only threats would have made them comply. He reckoned that this would have resulted in some resignations. In this case the manager was acting as a buffer between his X-style boss and his staff. The problem is that many managers are not able or willing to do this and treat their staff, in turn, in an X fashion.

2

DELEGATION

AMONG the comments made in Chapter 8 by some very unhappy employees, you may remember the statement: 'There is no delegation and the good work, I mean the interesting work, is kept by those above.' This comment demonstrates one of the reasons why managers must take delegation seriously and learn how to go about it. Juniors who are not allowed to do any more than the basic humdrum tasks soon become bored and disillusioned – and look for a job which offers more satisfaction.

There are a number of other reasons for taking delegation seriously:

- properly organised, it reduces pressure on the delegator and allows more time for managerial tasks such as forward planning, monitoring and recruiting new staff. The corollary is that senior, more experienced people can make their own working lives more interesting and rewarding by having the time for more challenging work.

- dependency on one or two people is reduced. This improves cover for sickness, holidays and other absences – and can improve service to customers.

- potential successors to the senior people are developed. This means that seniors can be promoted. The old fear that developing a successor creates a threat is at least counterbalanced by solving the common problem of not being able to promote someone because no successor is available.

- it reduces the need to recruit people at senior (and more experienced) levels. When the juniors are ready to move up the ladder their replacements will be at the lower end of the salary scale and normally easier to find.

- provided that it is well planned and executed, delegation improves the efficiency of a department (and, in turn, the company) – something which can only reflect favourably on the reputation of the managers.

Why don't people delegate?

Despite these substantial benefits, delegation is often neglected. Many reasons for this neglect can be found. The following are probably the most common ones:

'I tried it before and it was a disaster.'

'I have no staff who are capable of taking on more difficult work.'

'I have no time to delegate. It is quicker and easier to do the job myself.'

'It took me 10 years to learn this job and I don't see why these youngsters should expect to do it any faster.'

'The work we do here is too important for juniors to take on. If a mistake is made it could have serious consequences.'

'If I delegate I will lose touch with what is going on. By doing the work myself I can keep my finger on the pulse.'

All these fears and worries are entirely natural and understandable. They do not, however, stand up to close scrutiny and are not worthy of the truly professional manager. Let us look at them a little more closely.

It was a disaster before
This almost certainly means that the job of delegation was not done properly. Apart from that, if we never again attempted something which went wrong the whole world would grind to a halt. The first attempts to build flying machines were full of failures – some fatal.

No suitable staff
This means that the manager has no faith in his people. Is this because he recruited badly, has neglected to train his staff, lacks

confidence in himself, is so arrogant that he believes only he can do the job or all of these things? The manager himself is the only one who can solve the problem and the solution lies in his own hands.

No time
This is perhaps the most convincing excuse – at first glance. A disciplined on-job training (OJT) programme will be needed to break the vicious cycle of 'No time – no delegation – no time'. (Further details of how to organise OJT are given in Chapter 6, page 89.)

It is, of course, quicker for the experienced person to do a job than someone trying it for the first time. This was precisely the problem for the present experienced person when *he* first started. Someone delegated the work to him and gradually he acquired the skills to do it quickly. This process *must* be repeated at some point or the skill will disappear when the boss retires – or drops dead from heart failure caused by overwork and stress!

It took me 10 years to learn the job
This is one of the most common forms of self-delusion in business. The great bulk of the knowledge required for any job is acquired in the first year or two. After that the process of learning is slower – although no less important. This is what is meant by 'the learning curve' (see opposite). If a job really does take 10 years to learn (or 15 or 20 or whatever) then the sooner the boss starts delegating the better. If the boss leaves it too late he will not give the junior time to learn the job before he retires!

Errors could have serious consequences
There are hundreds of situations in business where errors can have serious consequences – sometimes quite dramatic ones too. That is why a young airline pilot works as a co-pilot with an experienced captain. The co-pilot actually flies the aeroplane but under supervision. There is no suggestion that commonsense precautions need be abandoned in a properly organised delegation programme.

I will lose touch
No manager needs to know everything in minute detail in order to keep his finger on the pulse. A combination of walking the job and *sensible* reports will keep him in control of the situation. One of the best forms of reporting (i.e. the least expensive and time-

The learning curve

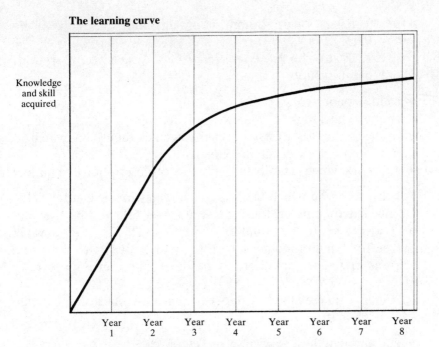

consuming) is 'by exception'. In other words, the manager is only informed if events indicate a trend away from the normal.

If, for example, orders are coming in at the expected rate of 10 each day then the manager need not be told. Should the rate drop to seven or eight a day (or rise to 12), then he needs to be informed as action may be needed. The acid test for reporting is the question of action. A report which requires no action as a result of receiving it is a waste of time and money. The job can be delegated and an exception reporting arrangement can be made at the same time.

Planning for delegation

All delegation should be carefully planned. The willy-nilly handing over of work to others is not delegation, it is dumping. And dumping work will lead to trouble unless you are very lucky.

A convenient place to start is you, the manager and what you do. First, list all the *managerial* tasks (such as forward planning) for which you have too little time. Include all the work that can only be completed by working late at night or at weekends. This list will tell you what you are neglecting, or in danger of neglecting.

After the delegation programme is implemented, these jobs will be better done.

Next, list all the *non-managerial* tasks which you carry out. These might include:

- routine paperwork
- routine checking
- jobs you have hung on to because you enjoy them – but which do not require your particular expertise
- and work which actually falls into the job description of a junior.

This list tells you which tasks are candidates for delegation. NB: Do not leave items off the list because you believe that they are beyond the skills and abilities of juniors. This is often a weak excuse for hanging on to something and anyway the skills and abilities of juniors are there to be developed and improved by delegation.

Finally, take a sheet of paper for each member of your team and write on it:

- age and length of service of the employee
- exactly what work they do now
- and your assessment of what additional work taken from your list of non-managerial tasks they could handle – *given adequate training*.

Writing this information down will force you to think about each person and to check that you know what they actually do. Managers are often surprised to find that subordinates do many more tasks then they realised. This becomes obvious when some-one leaves and, surprise surprise, a routine job suddenly does not get done. No one had ever really given a thought as to who did the job. It just happened every week in the normal way.

Now discuss what has been written down with the employee to check that the facts are right and to listen to what he has to say about your assessment of work he could take over. The result of this discussion will be a joint view of which of your responsibilities can be taken over by the employee. Normally managers are sur-prised at how willing juniors are to take on more responsibility and how confident they are of being able to do it. There are some exceptions and from time to time an employee with potential may need some confidence-building encouragement to move on to greater things.

Another important point to check is that any work earmarked for delegation should in some way benefit the employee concerned. Apart from adding interest and satisfaction to his job, the work will ideally be one of the stepping stones on a career development path leading to promotion. This will be an important incentive to the employee – and confirmation that you are not merely getting rid of a few tasks that you are fed up with.

The next stage is to draw up a delegation programme for each employee along the lines of this example.

DELEGATION PROGRAMME FOR CHARLIE BLOGGS

Task to be delegated	Training/experience required	Date for completion of delegation
1. Production requirement report	Analysis of customer orders	31 January
	Stock analysis	20 February
2. Attendance at monthly production planning meetings	Production planning techniques	15 March
	Visit to factory and warehouse – explanation of processes	20 March

Overall purpose: to take over sales/production liaison by 31 March

Persons responsible for training: Snooks, Brown and Green

Once agreed this programme must be adhered to *without fail* or the whole plan will collapse, with potentially serious effects on employee morale. Furthermore, no benefits will have been achieved for the manager, the employee or the company.

Dangers to be avoided

Managers must avoid falling into a number of traps. These include saying:

'I will do this when I am less busy.' (That day never comes.)

'I have no suitable staff.' (You have, or you can create them.)

'I am responsible so I must do it myself.' (The manager is always *accountable* but he can delegate the responsibility.)

'The work is too confidential for juniors.' (This is rare in practice and normally only involves sensitive personal data such as salaries.)

There are other dangers to be avoided, such as delegating the job, then interfering every five minutes. This merely destroys the confidence of the employee who should be given a chance to get on with it.

Then there are those managers who abandon the plan as soon as the employee makes a mistake. No one ever did a job without making mistakes – the employee will need patient understanding and support.

Another pitfall is insisting that the work is done in exactly the same way that you did it. One of the pleasures of doing a job is applying one's own ideas and imagination. Providing the result is the right one, the manager should permit an individual approach – which may actually work better than the manager's own way of doing it!

3

COMMUNICATION

WE have all heard comments like these:

'No one tells us anything round here.'

'How was I to know that no deliveries were to be made on Mondays?'

'I thought we were supposed to send out the invoices in duplicate.'

'I'm not sure what I'm supposed to do with these forms.'

'I don't know what they want.'

'No one told me.'

Remarks such as these are all symptoms of poor communication or none at all. They represent frustration, annoyance, feelings of hopelessness and similar emotions which can cause people to pack a job in. They are also symptomatic of situations in which mistakes occur and customers are let down.

The manager should ensure that everyone not only knows what is expected of them in terms of work to be done and standards required, but also in terms of every aspect of the work environment. Giving people the facts – the reasons why something is being changed, details of a new product, what the competition is doing, or whatever – brings several advantages. Work becomes more interesting and satisfying and commitment is encouraged. Well-informed people are in a better position to act intelligently when something unexpected occurs. And productivity, in turn, improves.

It is probably true that most of the foul-ups and many of the disputes that occur in industry can be traced back to faulty or absent communication. The manager who wishes to avoid problems and gain benefits by good communication must consider three key aspects:

- what to communicate
- when to communicate
- and how to communicate.

What to communicate

The things an employee needs to know about are *all* the things that will affect him personally or influence the way in which he does his job. They include all those factors listed by Herzberg as important in keeping the employee content (see Chapter 8, pages 123–4).

In practical terms, he needs to be kept informed of such things as:

- a new bonus scheme
- installation of new vending machines
- why the canteen will be closed for a few days
- a new design of payslip – and why
- revised safety rules – and why
- changes to holiday entitlements – and why
- and a new scheme for day release training.

The things which will influence how he does his job could include:

- what is expected of him in his work
- how he is doing
- prospects for promotion
- corporate plans
- new product launches
- a new marketing policy
- introduction of new equipment or machinery
- company, divisional and departmental results and achievements
- a new computer system
- the date for the annual stocktaking
- customer complaints – or praise
- and recruitment of new staff – who and when.

Some managers regard many of the subjects listed above as either 'confidential' or of no interest to the majority of employees (especially the juniors). This attitude can be very wrong. While there will always be a few items which should be kept under wraps for a time, in reality there is very little which needs to be kept from any employee however junior. Much of the secrecy beloved of some managers is no more than a form of ego trip. By keeping something to themselves these managers make themselves feel more important – members of an in-group who are superior to the rest.

In fact many employees will be interested in all that is going on, including corporate policy matters. Those who are not interested at first are often stimulated into taking an interest if understandable information is passed to them on a regular basis. Once interest is established, employees begin to feel part of the company and stop viewing it merely as a place where they work to earn some money. A good rule is 'If in doubt, communicate it.'

When to communicate

The short answer to the question 'When should they be told?' is 'As soon as you possibly can'. For instance, if a decision has been made to move the sales department to a new office in a building two miles away the employees concerned should be told promptly. These are several reasons for this.

Avoidance of rumours

Whenever something significant is being planned clues are bound to leak out and rumours will develop. Rumours are invariably damaging and have an unsettling effect on employees. The pessimists will assume the worst and pass on their fears in suitably graphic terms. Thus, the rumour will grow and become more and more unpalatable.

Such a case occurred in a company based in London. The company was moving to a new building and the staff had been informed of this fact. However no further information was provided, with the result that speculation soon led to rumours. One rumour had it that desks for typists and secretaries in the new building would be a cheap plastic variety with white tops.

The typists and secretaries were most upset by the story (which they firmly believed to be true) as they were loath to part with the smart wooden desks which had been a standard part of the furnishings hitherto. Management first became aware of the problem when a secretary who was being ticked off by her boss turned on him and demanded to know if the ticking off was all part of the plan to make the secretaries resign! The desks, it seemed, were another part.

The rumour was quickly scotched by a clear statement to all concerned that the existing desks would be retained and there had never been any intention of doing otherwise. It was later discovered that the rumour had started when a group of secretaries visiting the new building saw a number of white plastic 'desks' piled up in the entrance hall. They were in fact part of the equipment for the computer room.

Demonstrating trust

People are more likely to behave in an adult, responsible fashion if they are treated as such. Failure to inform employees has the opposite effect and gives rise to the feelings expressed in comments such as 'They don't care about us', 'We don't matter' or 'They don't trust us.' Once such attitudes are well entrenched they are very difficult to shift. They can, however, be avoided by good communication.

How to communicate

The methods by which management can communicate fall into three categories:

- face to face
- mass methods
- and via representatives.

Let us deal with the third of these first – because this method is the least reliable and is best disposed of at an early stage. While it may be convenient for management to provide information to shop stewards and similar representatives it is unlikely that the message will reach the employees in the same form as it left the management. The shop stewards may be tempted to use the information for 'political' purposes and deliberately distort it. For instance the less attractive aspects might be highlighted and benefits to employees played down or overlooked. This is particularly likely where company policy is to be explained. Shop stewards are not representatives of management and cannot be expected to be committed to every policy or policy change.

An additional problem in using representatives is that, in time, they (rather than the management) come to be seen by the shop floor as the bosses. It should be remembered that knowledge is power and the power needs to be in the right hands, working for the benefit of the company and *all* the employees.

Mass methods are the second best way to communicate and they have the advantage, generally, of being cheap and quick. Mass methods include notice boards, circulars and leaflets, letters included in pay packets, company newsletters and videos. The disadvantages of mass methods are that they tend to be impersonal – the notice board especially so – and it is not possible for questions to be asked. However using mass methods does ensure that the information provided is accurate.

Care needs to be taken with notice boards to see that they are in prominent positions (near the vending machines gives people an opportunity to see them) and also kept tidy and up to date. Many company notice boards are characterised by a jumble of tatty notes including details of the Christmas holiday break (two years ago) and the appointment of a new chairman (who has since retired). Such notice boards are rarely given serious attention.

Old notices should be regularly removed and the rest arranged in a tidy fashion. A useful tip is to use a special colour for notices which are particularly important. One company uses a 'red flash' system in which special notices are printed on paper with a red stripe across it. This attracts attention but it should only be used for genuinely significant information or the effect is lost.

Videos, if used, should be professionally prepared and dramatic. Thirty minutes of the chairman droning on and on is a first-class soporific and should be avoided. Cartoons, photographs, charts, diagrams and animated scenes with an enthusiastic voice-over are much more likely to make an impact.

By far the best way to communicate is the face-to-face method. This is the only way to have a chance of true communication because it allows information to pass in both directions. Face-to-face methods can include one-to-one situations, such as counselling, supervisor to section, manager to department or chief executive to the whole workforce.

A German company comprising about 50 staff places great importance on both communication and the face-to-face method. The head and founder of the company talks with his senior people every Friday afternoon and it is a company rule that the senior people (heads of departments) hold a 10- or 15-minute meeting every morning with their subordinates. The Friday meetings deal with such matters as levels of sales and income, problems and opportunities, priorities, workloads and staffing, staff training and budgets. The daily departmental meetings deal with similar subjects but generally in a shorter timespan. Day-to-day problems are discussed and action to be taken agreed.

By means of these meetings *all* the staff know what is going on, what is required, what progress is being made and so on. In addition, *all* the staff have an opportunity to air their opinions, explain their problems, put forward their ideas and ask questions. It is probably not a coincidence that staff losses (for reasons other than retirement, pregnancy and the like) are exceptional and give rise to a searching enquiry into what went wrong.

Communication techniques

Whichever communication method is chosen, the same techniques are required to make it successful. Simply sticking a notice on the notice board or giving a five-minute talk to a group of employees is not enough. Three factors need to be considered – preparation, transmission and assimilation. These three aspects will determine whether you communicate successfully or not.

Preparation
The preparation stage means taking the time to ensure that what you *say* is what is *heard*. It is unlikely that any two people will interpret a set of words in precisely the same way. Each person is influenced by their own background, training, environment, likes and dislikes and perspective. This is why certain people are called 'terrorists' by some and 'freedom fighters' by others. Exactly the same opposed thinking can occur in business situations and, to avoid misinterpretation, preparation must be made. Consider the importance of:

- being absolutely clear as to what it is you wish to communicate.
- how it is likely to be received by the various people present.
- where and when the information should be given and by whom.
- the type of people being addressed and, for example, how much detail they will need.

Even a few minutes careful thought before talking to a small group on a relatively simple subject can make all the difference between success and failure.

Transmission

The transmission aspect is equally important. This concerns the ways and means by which the message is given. Will an informal talk be more effective than a set-piece performance in the board room? Generally the following rules apply:

- be as informal as possible.
- keep it as brief as possible but don't miss anything out.
- speak slowly and clearly, avoiding unfamiliar jargon or technical terms.
- allow ample time for questions – and don't fail to answer them.
- use real life examples, slides, films, models or whatever to illustrate your message.

Assimilation

If the preparation has been sufficiently thorough and the transmission effective, it is almost certain that the final requirement – assimilation – will be successful. Whatever has been assimilated is what has been communicated – regardless of what you were *trying* to communicate.

There is only one way to check whether the right message has been assimilated and that is to ask questions. Remember also to encourage your audience to do so and, in addition, offer the option of talking to you privately if there is anything that anyone is unhappy about. Yes, this takes time but rather less than is needed to sort out the mess if someone has got it badly wrong.

Check your communication standards

Working through the following questions may give you some ideas on how to improve communication in your organisation:

- do employees communicate upwards (i.e. to their superiors) as much as you would wish? If not, why not?

- are your notice boards tidy and up to date?

- are sections and departments regularly briefed and informed of progress, targets, etc?

- can grievances be easily (and peacefully) aired?

- to what extent are employees informed about the progress of the company, its successes and failures?

- is there a way of publicly recognising good work?

- how easy is it for junior levels to talk to seniors? Is there a rank barrier?

- do *all* staff have a job description and a clear understanding of what is required of them?

- does everyone know what company objectives, policies and standards are?

- when did you last constructively discuss your immediate subordinates' work with them – individually?

- how often do you, your managers and supervisors 'walk the job'?

- how often do you ask employees for their opinions? Is there a regular arrangement for this to happen?

- do all your employees know how their work contributes to the business? Do you know?

- have you ever had a rumour problem? If so, what caused it?

4

MANPOWER PLANNING FOR THE SMALLER BUSINESS

IN Chapter 1 the technique known as manpower planning was mentioned as one used by the very large companies. The same principles can equally well apply to a small or medium-sized company but with a simplification of the process. Manpower planning has been defined as 'a strategy for the acquisition, utilisation, improvement and retention of an enterprise's human resources' (*Company Manpower Planning*, HMSO). A simpler definition would be 'a process to ensure that the organisation has the right number of the right people as needed from time to time'.

Manpower planning cannot work effectively in isolation. It must be an integral part of an overall business plan which includes consideration of the needs of the business in terms of finance, capital equipment, buildings and other resources. Planning the human resource element is only one, if a very important, part of the overall strategy. Having said that, in a number of small but expanding business the perceived need for more employees has given rise to questions such as 'Where are we going?' and 'How far can we expand without more machinery and space? These questions have in turn led to broader corporate thinking, triggered off in the first place by the need for more manpower and a realisation that this should be met in a controlled and planned way.

Some argue that planning must depend on forecasting and since no one can foretell the future then planning is a waste of time. In fact it is *because* no one can foretell the future that planning is essential. It must be accepted that forecasts are not prophecies and they will therefore always be wrong to some degree. But a plan, even one based on a best guess as to what will happen, means that the management have at least some chance of controlling their future. The alternative is to react at short notice to changing circumstances, hoping to get the best out of things before the next problem crops up. This is 'management by expediency', an expensive and inefficient method dominated by 'the slings and arrows of outrageous fortune' – or what your competition and others may choose to do.

What manpower planning involves

Essentially, the process divides into four parts:

- assessing where you are now
- deciding where you want to go
- forecasting what human resources you will need to reach your target
- and setting up and implementing a plan to acquire and retain the human resources.

This can be done in a very simple way – the simpler the better. Companies opting for manpower planning for the first time are better off with a fairly rudimentary plan which can be easily adjusted or added to as circumstances may dictate. In any case, no plan should be regarded as fixed, final and carved on tablets of stone. The process is best explained by taking a hypothetical company and seeing how they planned their future.

Sporticars Ltd

Sporticars, a company making hand-built cars for enthusiasts was founded 25 years ago by the present chairman. The company has developed a good reputation for its products and has grown to 100 employees. Sporticars believe that, with growing affluence, the potential market for enthusiasts' cars will double in the next five years. They are determined at least to maintain their 50 per cent share of this market and, if possible, to push up their share to 60 per cent.

The chairman has successfully negotiated the necessary finance for additional machinery and a lease has been signed for new factory premises conveniently situated next to the present factory. Everything is set for a sustained period of expansion and increased sales but the board still have one major problem to overcome – finding and keeping the manpower they will need.

As a first step the board have made an analysis of the present manpower position. They start with a look at the 'key employees' (i.e. those who play a significant role in the company). The resulting report is shown below.

Present manpower situation – Sporticars Ltd Key employees

Job title	Name	Age	Comments
Chairman	J. Smith	50	
Managing Director	B. Jones	45	
Production Director	A. Snooks	47	Handles all design work
Sales Director	K. Fastlane	62	3 years from retirement
Company Secretary	L. Bookwise	42	Qualified
Accountant	T. Moneybank	66	Over retirement age
Book-keeper	S. Avings	27	Keen, able but unqualified
Production Foreman	H. Ammer	39	
Chargehand	K. Black	40	
Chargehand	T. White	41	
Toolmaker	S. Teel	61	Approaching retirement
Toolmaker	B. Ronze	62	Approaching retirement
Salesman	A. Gogetter	27	Energetic but immature
Progress chaser	I. Findit	24	Bright, has engineering degree

Having examined the report, the board came to the following conclusions. The production director (Snooks) handles all the design work in addition to his other production duties. This is already a heavy burden on him and, since design is a vital aspect of the business, he needs support. After debate it was decided to recruit a qualified design engineer.

Old Fastlane, the sales director, is only three years from retirement. He has wide-ranging and important contacts and is much respected in the industry. He has no successor ready and able to take over. However he spoke well of young Gogetter who, although somewhat lacking in selling and interpersonal skills, is keen, intelligent and impatient to learn. It was decided to put Gogetter through a sustained training plan with a view to making him sales manager when Fastlane retires. At that time the managing director would take over responsibility for sales and Gogetter would report to him. In the meantime another salesman would be recruited.

Moneybank, the accountant, is already 66 years of age and has expressed a wish to retire. The book-keeper, Avings, is not qualified to take over the accountant's job – which is expected to expand in terms of complexity and volume of work. Recent tax legislation and EEC accounting rules are placing an ever-increasing burden on the accounting function.

The decision was made to place the accounting function under the company secretary who is not stretched in his present role. At the same time a computer system will be installed to handle all the book-keeping, costing and budgeting. The book-keeper will be offered training in computing with a view to becoming computer manager. It was also decided to recruit a junior (probably with some computer keyboard skills) to support the putative computer manager.

Both toolmakers were in sight of retirement and replacements would be needed. Toolmakers require a long period of training. In addition, the advanced engines and transmissions which the company is producing have already stretched the existing toolmakers' skills to the limit. After much heart-searching it was agreed that the time had come to start contracting toolmaking to a specialist company. This, it was expected, would be cheaper in the long run. Neither toolmaker would be replaced when they retired but the production foreman would be made responsible for liaison with the contractors. Arrangements would be made with the contractors for the foreman to familiarise himself with their production, quality control and testing system.

The progress chaser Findit was clearly under-utilised. His engineering knowledge was not fully used in progress chasing and it was felt that he would resign if a more promising position was not found for him. The board decided to defer a decision on his future until the manpower planning process was a little more advanced – bearing in mind that Findit was a valuable resource held, temporarily, in reserve.

The board now examined an analysis of the general workforce. The report they received is shown below. The report caused some concern in the board room because it clearly showed that a substantial proportion of the skilled people were in the upper age bracket. Although this meant that they were less likely to leave the company than their younger colleagues, it also meant that a significant number would retire over a relatively short period – and before very long.

Present manpower position – Sporticars Ltd
Workforce – non key

Job title	Age up to 30	31–50	50+	Comments
Machine operators	15	10	10	28.5% over 50
Upholsterers	2	2	11	73.3% over 50
Painters	6	1	8	53.3% over 50
Sales clerks	2	2	—	
Storekeeper	1	—	1	
Delivery drivers	2	—	—	
Canteen staff	—	—	2	
Gatekeepers	—	—	2	
Typists	4	1	1	
Labourers	—	3	—	
Total	32	19	35	
%	37.2	22.1	40.7	

It was agreed that there was little opportunity to replace the manual skills with mechanical processes, particularly in the case of the upholsterers whose dexterity with leather seating and linings made a vital contribution to the quality standards on which the business depended. The local technical college turned out a regular flow of young people suitable for training as machine operators, and painters could be taught in-house from scratch, but

upholsterers were a different matter. There was no training establishment in the area which catered for this skill and long practice
was needed to become proficient.

It was decided to set up a high-quality apprenticeship scheme
and to ask the local technical college for support. The managing
director would be responsible for this exercise. Findit, the progress
chaser, would be offered the job of helping him in the initial stages
and subsequently taking over responsibility for all technical
training.

This would make better use of Findit's engineering knowledge
and give him a more challenging and satisfying job. He would then
be sent on an external course on training management at one of the
business schools. And progress chasing would be offered to one of
the machine operators who had shown a higher degree of initiative
and intelligence than the average. This person would understudy
Findit for a few weeks to learn the job.

The rest of the workforce presented no apparent problems but
it was agreed that the sales clerks should be trained in telephone
technique to improve relations with customers, and the typists
should be trained in word-processing to improve productivity and
reduce the need to find additional typists as the work expanded.

The logistics

Having made its decision, the board now needed to set up a plan
for implementation which would take into account the various
time limitations and the estimated natural wastage which would
occur. Based on previous history, it was decided that about 25 per
cent of the apprentices recruited for the technical jobs would not
make it to the end of the course. Most of the leavers would go in the
first year of the course.

It was also estimated that in five years' time the number of
technical staff would need to be double the present number. A
chart was drawn up for each of the technical jobs showing the
numbers involved. The table for the upholsterers is shown on the
next page.

It was fully appreciated that the numbers were based on forecasts. Although retirements could be reliably determined, wastage
was another matter. There was also the possibility of unexpected
losses as a result of illness or sudden death. However the table
provided a framework and, at worst, order-of-magnitude figures

Upholsterers – recruitment and training plan

	Existing	Recruits	Estimated wastage	Retirements	Year end number
Year 1	15	10	3	1	21
Year 2	21	6	2	2	23
Year 3	23	6	2	2	25
Year 4	25	6	2	1	28
Year 5	28	6	2	2	30

showing what provision needed to be made for the selection and induction of recruits and the space and equipment required for them. It would be Findit's job to keep an eye on actual results and to revise the recruitment and training programme as necessary to stay on target.

The final job for the board was to summarise the whole plan in a form which could be used both to communicate it to the whole workforce and to monitor progress. The diagrammatic plan is shown on the next page.

Sporticars Ltd will no doubt find that various problems, large and small, will crop up as time goes by. The plan may need regular revision and it would be desirable to have a number of contingency actions prepared in advance. These contingency plans, which will help to reduce the risk of failure, might include action to be taken in the event of:

- the death of a key person
- another employer opening up nearby and attracting people to them
- failure to gain the number of skilled technicians required
- sales forecasts significantly wrong
- and unexpected cash flow problems.

It is impossible for a company to make provision for every

191

Sporticars Ltd – manpower plan as at 1 February 1989

Action	Purpose	Timing	Responsible person	Comments
1. Recruit design engineer	To relieve production director	Immediate	Snooks/Bookwise	
2. Training plan for salesman (Gogetter)	To become sales manager	Completion in 3 years	Fastlane/Bookwise	MD will take over role of sales director
3. Company secretary to take over accounting function	To replace retiring accountant	Completion by 1 May	Bookwise/Moneybanks	
4. Book-keeper to take over computer systems	Computerisation of book-keeping	Training to start March	Bookwise	Company secretary and computer manager designate will select and arrange computer installation
5. Junior to be recruited for accounts section	Assistant to computer manager	Immediate	Bookwise/Avings	
6. Toolmakers to be advised of contract plan	To prepare for switch to contract system	Immediate	MD	Toolmakers to be assured of job security until retirement
7. Production foreman to liaise with contractors	To ensure quality, timeliness and preferred customer status	When contract agreed	Snooks	Familiarisation plan to be arranged with contractors by MD
8. Set up apprenticeship scheme	To provide future skilled workforce	First entrants at end of college year	Bookwise/Findit	
9. Progress chaser to take over as technical training manager	To organise and supervise apprenticeship scheme	As soon as replacement is trained	Bookwise/Findit	*Note: This plan will be regularly reviewed and implementation monitored by the MD. Any revisions which are necessary will be published promptly.*

problem which may come up but a pre-agreed strategy for dealing with the more serious ones can prevent panic-stricken and ill-considered action being taken at short notice.

Manpower planning in practice

As you will notice Sporticars' plan was not merely a list of recruitment needs. It also incorporated:

- development of individuals (e.g. the progress chaser)
- new technology (e.g. the computer)
- alternative production methods (contracting out the toolmaking)
- re-allocation of responsibilities (sales to the MD and accounting to the company secretary)
- and innovation (the apprenticeship scheme).

In real life (from which much of the Sporticars example is taken) manpower planning tends to lead to such changes. Management thinking is frequently stirred up and profitable ideas are generated.

In the example the board first reviewed existing manpower resources. And it was assumed that apprentices could be recruited from the local technical college and other required people could be found. In real life the situation may not be so easy and external sources of people should be realistically reviewed.

It is also wise to seek a balance between external recruiting and internal promotions in order to avoid upsetting existing staff on the one hand, and suffering the effects of inbreeding on the other. The aspirations and potential of existing employees for development and promotion need to be ascertained. Similarly, you need to consider the external position in terms of:

- output from schools and colleges
- local unemployment levels
- actions of other employers
- local skills and traditions
- and the lead-time to recruit people.

The manpower plan may reveal that some existing exployees will not be needed as time goes by (e.g. as a result of abandoning an unsuccessful product or the introduction of new technology). In such cases the last resort is redundancy, which is costly and damaging to employee morale, and in the author's opinion wholly immoral. There are alternatives such as voluntary early retirement, re-training for other jobs in the company and natural wastage, or a combination of these.

Manpower planning is therefore a powerful tool of management. It is more a process than a plan, and one which can ensure both that the company has the right kind of people and that appropriate opportunities are created for them.

5

A WIDER VIEW OF DISCIPLINE

THE word 'discipline' conjures up different pictures. One person's thoughts may turn to a slave galley or a flogging on a ship in Nelson's time. Other, more gentle souls may think of telling off an employee who is late for work while others may have visions of rigid ranks of soldiers on parade. To consider discipline fully, we need to take in wider considerations of how people work and the effects on efficiency and employee welfare.

Having a system – and using it

Working to a system is easier and more effective than working in a muddle. While everyone who works in a muddle will grumble about the mistakes, duplication of work and frustration of it all, it is rare for the same people to be either willing or able to do anything about it.

This is one of the manager's responsibilities – to work out a sensible system for doing things and to ensure that the employees stick to it. A good system will have the following features:

- it will be as simple and straightforward as possible.
- there will be a good and well-understood reason for every part of it.
- it will be designed in consultation with the people who use it and anyone affected by it.
- it will be written down in narrative and/or diagrammatic form so that it can be referred to and used in training new recruits.

Avoiding silly rules

Silly rules are those which serve no useful purpose or may be damaging. A good look at company rules can yield dividends in getting rid of irritants to the staff and time-wasting activities for supervisors and managers.

The types of rule which need reconsideration are:

- restrictions on dress. (These may be too rigid or limiting and cause resentment.)

- entrances for the exclusive use of certain employees. (Such restrictions cause bad feeling and avoidable status worries.)

- requirements to obtain permission from a senior level for minor matters. (The time lost and the frustration can be costly – and VIPs who insist on approving the issue of another split pin or packet of paper clips look as silly as the rule.)

- out-of-date requirements. What may have been a sensible rule 30 years ago may now be a nonsense.

- incomprehensible rules. Any rule written in the sort of language used by the local council to publicise the bye-laws relating to allotments is a candidate for scrapping or simplification.

Rules which are understandable and have a clear purpose are more likely to be followed – without the need for close supervision of the employees.

Creating a 'culture of discipline'

A 'user-friendly' discipline will have been achieved when employees say with some pride, 'This is the way we do things here', or, 'We prefer such and such here'. This context will also have a marked absence of rules for all but essential matters such as safely and to meet legal requirements. Such a culture is achievable – more easily in the small company than the large company.

You could start by setting up a small committee representing all levels of employees. It should meet regularly to recommend working methods, administrative systems and any other ways of creating an attractive yet ordered environment.

Other requirements include regular and easy contact between managers and employees with opportunity for informal discussion, and a suggestion scheme in which suggestions are considered and evaluated not by management alone but also by employees' representatives.

It is from such arrangements that discipline develops without any need for long lists of rules or sanctions to enforce them. Having to enforce the rules means that management has failed to work *with* the employees or to communicate effectively. A wider view of discipline than the big stick can help in keeping good staff.

6

THE LEGAL ASPECTS

THE law relating to employment is constantly evolving. New legislation and, in Europe, the influence of European Community directives present employers with an ever-changing situation. In addition, in countries with systems of law such as that in the UK, legislation is subject to interpretation by the courts – and sometimes reinterpretation on appeal in higher courts.

The prospect of a single market in Europe in 1992 has raised ideas of a single legal framework which will include a number of clauses on employees' rights. While a battle, started in 1989 over the need for a unification of employment law, rages on between the European Employers' Federation and the European Commission, employers are left with the problem of working out what the law is. They are also faced with the problem of guessing what the law will be in the future – and how the courts will interpret it.

Large companies which can afford to employ legal staff and full-time personnel professionals can expect to be guided by them on the legal requirements to be met – and how to go about it. The smaller company, unable to employ its own experts, must ensure that it is aware of and uses external sources of reliable advice. Fortunately, for companies in the UK, there are a number of such sources and the advice they give is both sound and often free of charge.

These sources include the Advisory Conciliation and Arbitration Service (ACAS), the Institute of Personnel Management, the Industrial Society and the Department of Employment (see page 202 for addresses). ACAS provides a number of clear concise booklets and handbooks which include the following:

Individual employment rights

Employing people – a handbook for small firms

198

Employment policies

Redundancy arrangements

Disciplinary practice and procedures in employment.

The Industrial Society runs regular seminars and courses on aspects of employment law including such topics as the effect of European decisions on UK employment legislation, discrimination, health and safety and so on. It also has an information service.

The Department of Employment (DOE) offers a series of booklets on employment legislation. These are free of charge and can be obtained from any DOE office.

As a minimum, companies need to be aware of the legal provisions relating to the following:

- contracts of employment
- health and safety at work
- disciplinary and grievance procedures
- discrimination and equal pay
- trade unions (and the rights of individual union members)
- industrial tribunals
- unfair dismissal and dismissal for long-term ill-health
- redundancy and redundancy payments
- the rights of pregnant women (e.g. maternity leave)
- statutory sick pay
- time off for public duties (e.g. Justices of the Peace)
- and race relations.

Simply reading the newspapers is not enough to keep up to date with the latest position on these topics. Close contact with the sources of advice already listed is essential. An example of a change requiring up-to-date knowledge is the 1988 Employment Bill which had an impact on the Sex Discrimination Act (1975) and other employment legislation. The effect is to provide greater equality of employment opportunity for women and (partly in response to an EC directive) tidies up the rules on redundancy entitlements.

Another way of keeping up with this type of change is to use one of the 'ring binder' services offered by certain publishers. An example is Sweet & Maxwell's *Employment Law Manual* which includes an updating service. There is, of course, a charge for these services but the information provided could save costs many times greater. And it is comforting to know that changes which may affect you will be notified automatically with an explantion of case-law developments.

There are also a number of guides to employment law. Among them, for example, is Croner's *Guide to Absence*. These guides are written for the layman and can be a useful source of reference. The golden rule is, 'If in any doubt, check first before acting.'

7

WHERE TO LOOK FOR HELP

Further reading

Readers who wish to study some of these subjects in more detail may find the following books helpful.

INTERVIEWING:
Interviews: Skills and Strategy by John Courtis (Institute of Personnel Management)

TESTING METHODS:
Judging People by D. Mackenzie Davey and Marjorie Harris (McGraw-Hill)
This book gives an explanation of everything from astrology to psychological tests.

DISCIPLINE:
I'd Like a Word With You and *Managing Problem People*. (Both Video Arts booklets: Video Arts Ltd, Dumbarton House, 68 Oxford Street, London W1N 9LA   Tel: 081–367 7288

COUNSELLING:
Can you spare a moment? (Video Arts booklet)

ABSENTEEISM:
Fit for Business by Matthew Archer (Mercury)
Absence – a Croner's guide to the legal aspects

LEADERSHIP SKILLS:
Leadership is Not a Bowler Hat by Peter J. Prior, CBE (David & Charles)
This is a brief (64-page) statement of the successful methods used by Peter Prior in his position as chairman of the successful and innovative Hereford cider-makers Bulmer's.

There are also the various publications from the Advisory Conciliation and Arbitration Service (ACAS) and the Department of Employment (DOE) mentioned on pages 108–9.

Organisations which can help

ACAS
Clifton House, 83–117 Euston Road, London NW1 2RB   Tel: 071–388 5100. ACAS also has regional offices throughout the UK.

British Institute of Management
Management House, Cottingham Road, Corby, Northants NN17 1TT   Tel: 0536–204222

Business Information Service
University of Warwick (Library), Gibbetts Hill Rd, Coventry CV4 7AL   Tel: 0203–523051

Department of Employment
See local telephone directory.

Financial Times Business Information Service
126 Jermyn Street, London SW1Y 4UJ   Tel: 071–925 2323

Industrial Society
3 Carlton House Terrace, London SW1Y 5DG   Tel: 071–839 4300

Institute of Personnel Management
35 Camp Road, Wimbledon, London SW19 4UW   Tel: 081–946 9100

Small Firms Service
Ebury Bridge House, Ebury Bridge Road, London SW1W 8QD   Tel: 071–730 8451   Also at regional offices.

Training courses

Regular courses are run by the Industrial Society on a wide range of subjects and The Institute of Personnel Management also offers courses including one on 'Selecting the Right Candidate'.

The videos produced by Video Arts Ltd and Rank Training can be very helpful. Rank Training can be contacted at: Cullum House, North Orbital Road, Denham, Bucks UB9 5HL   Tel: 0895–834142.

INDEX